# WETLANDS

## *The Web of Life*

# WETLANDS
## *The Web of Life*

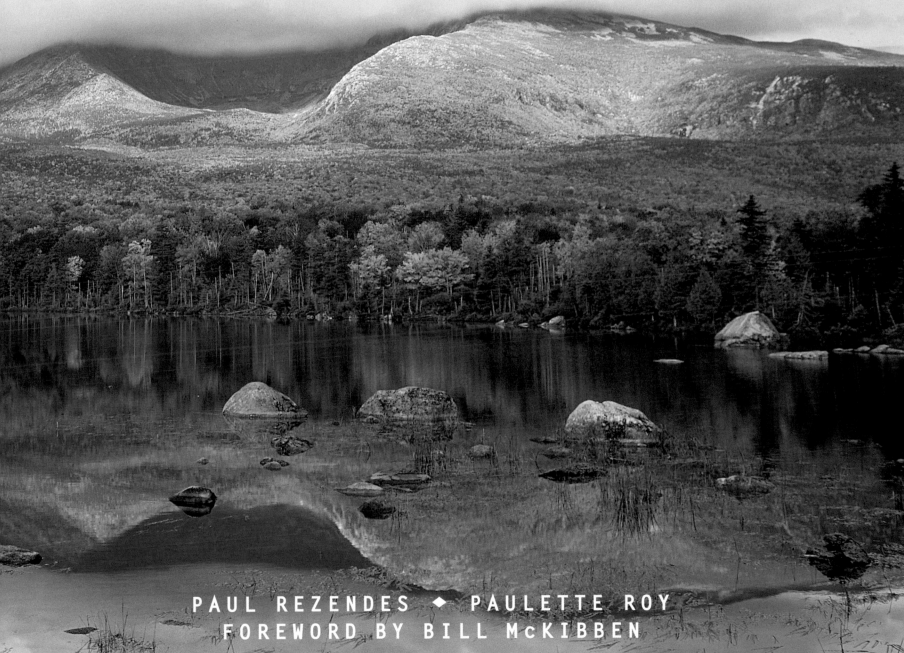

**PAUL REZENDES** ◆ **PAULETTE ROY**
FOREWORD BY BILL McKIBBEN
PHOTOGRAPHS BY PAUL REZENDES

A SIERRA CLUB BOOK

*To our mothers, Beatrice and Julie*

Many thanks to the countless people who have contributed to the process of creating this book.
A special thanks to Gary Chassman and Julie Stillman of Verve Editions for insisting that we write this book
together, for their dedication and commitment to the book, and for their support and encouragement along the way;
to Bill Harvey for his wonderful design and willingness to listen to our input regarding the presentation of
photographs; to our scientific reviewers Diane Boretos, Scott Jackson and Mark Kern for their meticulous scrutiny of
the draft manuscript and thoughtful comments; and to Mark Picard for reviewing the photography chapter. Thanks
also to the many folks in the National Parks, National Wildlife Refuges, U.S. Fish and Wildlife Service, Sierra Club,
The Nature Conservancy and dozens of state, local, and private conservation and environmental organizations who
willingly and cheerfully provided information about and directions to many of the locations we photographed. Their
assistance was invaluable and is deeply appreciated. And finally, to our families, friends, clients, and students who
have put up with, among other things, our lack of availability or delayed responses while working under deadline.
We are grateful, from the bottom of our hearts, for their generosity of spirit and belief in our work.

Developed and produced by

Burlington, Vermont
Gary Chassman & Julie Stillman

Designed by Bill Harvey

© 1996 by Paul Rezendes and Paulette Roy

The Sierra Club, founded in 1892 by John Muir, has devoted itself to the study and protection of the earth's scenic and ecological resources —
mountains, wetlands, woodlands, wild shores and rivers, deserts and plains. The publishing program of the Sierra Club offers books to the public as a
nonprofit educational service in the hope that they may enlarge the public's understanding of the Club's basic concerns. The point of view expressed
in each book, however, does not necessarily represent that of the Club. The Sierra Club has some sixty chapters coast to coast, in Canada, Hawaii,
and Alaska. For information about how you may participate in its programs to preserve wilderness and the quality of life, please address inquiries to
Sierra Club, 85 Second Street, San Francisco, CA 94105.

Printed by Palace Press International Hong Kong

10  9  8  7  6  5  4  3  2  1

*Library of Congress Cataloging-in-Publication Data*
Rezendes, Paul.
Wetlands: the web of life/Paul Rezendes, Paulette M. Roy.
p.   cm.
ISBN 0-87156-878-0 (paper); 851-9 (cloth)
1. Wetland ecology—North America.   2. Wetlands—North America.
3. Wetland ecology—North America—Pictorial works.   4. Wetlands—North America—Pictorial works.
I. Roy, Paulette M.   II.Title.
QH102.R48   1996
574.5'26325'097—dc20                    96-14942

# CONTENTS

Five or six years ago, beavers built a dam about twenty feet from my house. It transformed the streambed behind—flattened it out into a murky and shallow pond. At first I missed the gurgle of the creek, and anyway I think I shared the hardwired prejudice against murk, against slime, against mud. Against mosquitoes.

It didn't take long, though. Soon the flowers were shooting up in the sunlight coming through the dying trees and in the mud trapped by the dam; soon the red-winged blackbirds were arriving by the squadron to take up residence; soon the heron was regally flying in each night, his prehistoric and unlikely glide a deep marker of timelessness. Soon my daughter was painting herself with deep black mud. Soon the martins were sucking down bugs, the woodpeckers knocking with all their persistent optimism. And always the beavers, their orange teeth still visible in the dusky light, coming out for another night's work.

Not everyone has the good fortune to live so near a wetland. (Too many people, unfortunately, live in homes built on top of former wetlands, a circumstance of which they are reminded in the damper springs. But there's little romance in wading through the basement trying to figure out if the water's come up high enough to wreck the furnace.) But now Paul Rezendes and Paulette Roy offer — in word and especially in picture — each of us the chance to overcome our ignorance and antipathy to appreciate these damp and buzzing places.

I've been to some of the places they photograph — the 2,000-year old cypresses of the Black River for instance, the oldest things living east of the bristle-cone pines. Their riparian redoubt — guarded by reptile, serenaded by ibis, draped with Spanish moss — is as otherworldly as any place on the continent, at least if you associate "worldly" with concrete. The salt marshes of the New England coast, changing minute by minute with the lap and retreat of the sea. The quaking bogs of the boreal realms, with their floating mats of peat. And I've seen these places in the many seasons: early ice, the first sheets spreading out from small hummocks; black ice, like a windowpane for watching the turtles below; thick ice, perfect for skating endless figures around the snaggy trunks; early spring in the forest, when the wood frogs never cease their quacking from the tiny vernal pools; full spring, when the whole range of trills and belches ring out from the marshes; summer, when it's all buzz and whine and late-night slap of beavertail; autumn, when the damselflies glide slowly by in the last warmth for months to come.

But in all that time I've never thought so clearly about wetlands as Rezendes and Roy — understood them so fully as one of the key meeting places of life. A bazaar, if you will, where all mix and mingle, me with my blood to feed the mosquitoes, who in turn nourish the fish, who at some great remove help power my hand to swat against the sting. And that is just one of a billion transactions in this marketplace, this intersection of water and air and light that through the various happy mechanics of photosynthesis and evolution manages to add interest to every transaction.

Only when one has absorbed such an image — opened oneself to both the scientific and the spiritual matter contained in a book like this — is it possible to think soundly about the future of these places. Otherwise they will be what they have been throughout history: inconvenient puddles waiting to be drained and planted with corn or homes or malls. For most of human history, it was understandable when we treated swamps with disdain: for one thing, the unobservant did not yet know how central these damp spots were to the fabric of our ecology. And for another, we were few in number and the marshes were still vast. Now that has changed, and with it, slowly, have come shifts in attitude. We're beginning to realize that, as is often the case, that which we held most in contempt we now must cherish most dearly. In this country we've passed legislation to prevent "net loss of wetlands," and it has stirred controversy — some in Congress or the administration seek each year to erode the protection, for some short-term gain. But a hundred constituencies — the duck hunters, the clean-water drinkers, the bird-watchers, the global-warming fearers, the species-counters — understand more and more the centrality of these places.

May Rezendes and Roy add to that momentum. With these spectacular images they make "wetlands" — a term that has always sounded rather technical — a word that stirs the heart. May they do for Okefenokee what Ansel Adams did for Tuolomne. Someday, surely, we will love these low and damp places as much as the lofty, cold, and granite ones. Maybe even more, since our very bodies are wetlands too, warm and ticking, buzzing, growing, blooming. Mysterious and glorious.

Bill McKibben

Almost anywhere you live there exists some sort of wetland not too far away. Whether it's a tiny stream, a roaring river, a coastal salt marsh, or the great Everglades, wetlands undeniably shape our landscape and have a profound impact on our lives. Wetlands are a very visible subject these days, increasingly sharing the headlines with other environmental issues. Often bound up in controversy, wetlands are argued and fought over, coveted or loathed, depending on your perspective of what is "appropriate" land use. Any way you look at it, the topic is attracting lots of attention.

This book is a journey in photographs and words through each of the many and varied types of wetlands: inland marshes, coastal wetlands, peatlands, swamps, lakes, ponds, rivers, and streams. Each chapter provides a description and definition of a particular wetland type and explains the ecology of that wetland—how the elements in that ecosystem interconnect and interact with each other, as well as with the environment as a whole. The final chapter offers an inside perspective on the unique challenges of photographing wetlands. From sharing philosophical ideas on the "art of seeing" and creativity to providing practical information on equipment and photographic techniques, the chapter illustrates the photographer's approach to capturing the subtlety and nuance of these fragile environments. We hope this exploration of wetlands will increase your awareness of the importance, beauty, and drama of these highly valuable, life-producing ecosystems.

What comes to mind when people think of wetlands? One of the more common visual images is of a marsh, with an array of thick, lush plants, such as water lilies, cattails, or tussock sedge. Others might have a less specific image, and see wetlands generally as places of profound beauty bordering on the mystical. Others may view wetlands as an integral part of their being, a powerfully productive force shaping their lives.

Perhaps a totally different scene is evoked for some, that of an unproductive piece of land breeding mosquitoes, frogs, and snakes, some of which might even be poisonous and a threat to human life. Best then to fill the place in, farm it, build on it, get some use out of it. This type of outlook, coupled with greed and ignorance, has contributed to the loss of over one-half of the original wetlands in the United States, nearly 12 million acres of which were lost between the mid-1950s and the mid-1970s alone.

How have we arrived at such different views? To answer this question, there needs to be a process of self-examination that explores the depths of who we are versus who we *think* we are. Our relationship with wetlands is not separate from how we perceive ourselves. Our whole notion of who we are dictates our sense of place in the universe and how we relate to wetlands and all the creatures with whom we share the planet. Unless we have this understanding, we will only have partial success in saving our wetlands, no matter how hard we fight for legislation to stop their demise.

Through the eons, people have inherited many different self-perspectives, but let's examine two that might be useful. When the Europeans came to the shores of North America, they brought with them a sense of superiority, of being civilized, righteous people of God. They encountered a land that, to their eyes, was wild and untamed. They lived in fear of the dark woods and swamps. Predators, like mountain lions and wolves, were thought to be possessed by the devil. These wild beasts and their kingdom had to be controlled, conquered, and defeated. The colonists' view of the world gave them dominion over nature, keeping them separate and apart from it. They constantly battled against it. For them, security, both physical and emotional, meant power, domination, and control over nature. Unfortunately, some people still share this world view 500 years later.

The indigenous people living here when the Europeans arrived had a dramatically different world view. They perceived themselves as an extension of the land and the animals, as a part of nature, where their needs were not separate from the needs of the frogs and snakes or the deep dark forests and swamps. To the contrary, what was happening to the forests and its creatures was happening to them. From this perspective, being in harmony with the environment, living attuned and sensitive to nature, provides security.

There are many people today who share this more holistic perspective of themselves and their environment. In fact, we have only to breathe to be reminded that we are all intricately connected. Inhale and you inhale the breath of millions of living beings that have existed over millions of years. We are not separate from those beings whose lives and deaths have created the gases in our atmosphere that make life on earth possible.

It is an indisputable fact of life that we all take products from nature, whether from the sea, the forest, or the wetlands. How we go about doing this, however, depends on how we perceive ourselves in relation to the world around us. The attitude that "I can do what I want in my own backyard" is essentially a 1990s version of the European colonists' land ethic. With that view, it's not hard to see why we are destroying our forests and wetlands at an alarming rate. Many people simply do not realize that their backyard is connected to everyone else's and that it is not possible to do something "just" in "my backyard."

How then do we get to truly know nature, to understand our place in and relationship with the world so that we can act appropriately? If we examine our approach to learning in general, one hindrance is that fundamentally we seek knowledge solely through our intellect. We put "things" into categories, separate, label, and store them away to recall later. We look at a marsh, for example, and identify the different plants, animals, minerals, etc. We now think we know this marsh. If we stop there, however, all we have really learned is how to label the components. We need to fully embrace what the marsh is, to be aware of all its interconnections and relationships, all its life-support systems, and what it in turn supports. Instead of using just the intellect to learn, we might try wading into the marsh and feeling for young cattail shoots deep in the black muck. Our nostrils fill with the distinctive marsh scent of gases released by the movement of our feet. Grasping the cattail shoots at their roots, we feel their grip on life. As we cut the shoots from the roots, they give a part of themselves to us. We gather, clean, and cook the shoots, and in eating them, they awaken a new sense of texture, smell, and taste that we hadn't experienced before. Now we are getting to know cat-

tails. We have connected with them in an intimately more profound way than simply having the knowledge of the label.

Not all of us will have the opportunity to gather cattail shoots and experience their delightful aroma and taste. However, we can all get to know nature beyond simply labeling and categorizing, if we are willing to expand our way of knowing through using all of our senses. Listen to the insects, touch the water, smell the flowers, observe the web of life all around us.

As we become more intimate with nature, we begin also to understand ourselves better, and how the interconnections between living organisms include the human species. It is essential to understand and embrace all of who we are. To grasp this understanding with our whole being, to be intimate with the interrelationships of all life, is to truly change the way we perceive who we are and how we see the world around us.

We've been discussing different perspectives of nature and wetlands in general and our relationship with them, in hopes of giving you the opportunity to think about (or begin to develop) your own relationship with wetlands. We would be remiss in our task if we didn't also provide information to help define what a wetland is. According to the U.S. Fish and Wildlife Service (USFWS), technically, wetlands are "lands transitional between terrestrial and aquatic systems where the water table is usually at or near the surface, or the land is covered by shallow water." Most people are already familiar with wetlands, not by definition, perhaps, but by the common names we use to describe them, such as marshes, swamps, bogs, fens, mires, muskegs, bottomlands, small ponds, sloughs, potholes, river overflows, mud flats, and wet meadows, among others. Other types of wetlands discussed in this book are considered to be deepwater habitats, defined as "permanently flooded lands lying below the deepwater boundary of wetlands." These deepwater habitats include lakes, rivers, bays, and reservoirs.

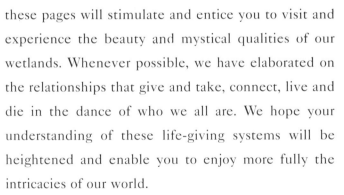

Though there are distinctive terms for different types of wetlands, these ecosystems tend to meld one into the other: a marshy area along the far side of a lake or a shrub swamp bordering a slow-moving stream. You will notice this in many of the photographs. We will distinguish as many different types of wetlands as possible, while still exploring the interplay of all the different components of these systems.

Our intention with this book is to develop an understanding of and appreciation for the complexities of our wetland systems. Our approach reflects a holistic perspective of the environment and emphasizes the interdependency among water, plants, animals, and humans. We welcome the opportunity to share with others a perspective of self that is not separate from nature. We hope the photographs on these pages will stimulate and entice you to visit and experience the beauty and mystical qualities of our wetlands. Whenever possible, we have elaborated on the relationships that give and take, connect, live and die in the dance of who we all are. We hope your understanding of these life-giving systems will be heightened and enable you to enjoy more fully the intricacies of our world.

# INLAND

# MARSHES

*Saving marshlands*

*and redwoods*

*does not need ... justification*

*any more than does opposing*

*callousness and vandalism.*

- René Dubos

ost of our time outdoors, whether taking photographs or teaching natural-history subjects, is spent at wetland edges or on a body of water itself. Many mornings, before dawn, find us gazing out meditatively over a fog-shrouded marsh, captured by its stillness, waiting for the first hint of light. A faint glow appears in the east and slowly begins to intensify. There is a silence, deep and timeless, accentuated by the movement of the canoe slicing slowly through still water. Two paddles dip quietly, working together without thought, like the school of fingerlings swimming below. The ground fog carries the sharp bark of a coyote, which ascends to a howl, then is joined by others. In the distance, a barred owl's faint call seems to answer the coyote chorus. The first rays of sun enter the marsh slowly, gently pushing us from our reverie into the day's work.

Inland marshes make up the most widely and evenly distributed wetlands in North America. They are visually exciting and particularly diverse, ranging from the saw grass marshes of the Everglades and wetland prairies of the Okefenokee (with alligators) to the northern marshes (with moose). Because of their high levels of beneficial nutrients, marshes are considered to be among the most productive ecosystems on earth. They

**Wetlands Marsh, *Birch Hill, Massachusetts*** *The dried sedges and grasses of this marsh glow in the early morning light of late fall. Wetlands often exist as continuums, where marshes blend into ponds and swamps, creating diverse habitats that can support a wide variety of wildlife species, from the occasional moose and great blue heron to resident populations of muskrats and amphibians.*

***OVERLEAF:* Okefenokee National Wildlife Refuge, *Georgia*** *This small marsh is surrounded by evergreen bay forests of primarily sweet bay, red bay and loblolly bay which make up about 6% of the larger Okefenokee Swamp. 55% of the remaining area is covered by marshes, waterways, and small lakes, 21% by cypress swamps, 12% by islands, and the last 6% is made up of swamp tupelo, red maple, and dahoon holly.*

sustain an extremely wide variety of plant communities, which in turn support the prolific wildlife activity within this wetland ecosystem.

Soil, water, and vegetation are the main components by which we begin to categorize inland marshes. They often have a combination of organic muck and/or mineral-rich soils of sand, silt, and clay. Some marshes form in depressions that collect enough water to support water-loving (hydrophytic) plants. Others form in shallows along the edges of rivers, ponds, and lakes. Many inland freshwater marshes are inundated with water year-round. Water levels may vary, from a few inches in a shallow marsh to five or six feet in a deep marsh. However, some marshes, like prairie potholes, may dry out completely during the course of the year. Wet mead-

ows, often resembling grasslands, are usually drier than other marshes, though they can be intermittently or temporarily flooded. For most of the year, wet meadows are without standing water, though the water table is often just below the surface, causing the soil to remain saturated. Wet meadows generally have a higher soil fertility than other marshes.

Plant communities of the inland marsh require a supply of oxygen and fairly high nutrient levels compared to other wetlands, such as peatlands. Marshes are open systems where there is an influx and outflow of water. This exchange is necessary to support the various organisms living in the marsh.

The inland marsh ecosystem generally supports soft-stemmed herbaceous plants. Shallow marshes provide

**Wetland Prarie, *Okefenokee National Wildlife Refuge, Georgia*** *The Okefenokee exemplifies the type of marsh often referred to as wetland prairie. They are commonly covered by one to three feet of water, and underlain by peat beds that average five to ten feet deep. The prairies include areas of open water as well as floating mats of vegetation or aquatic plants. Clumps of higher ground can develop on the accumulated peat to form small islands called houses or cypress heads.*

*"Marshes are open systems where there is an influx and outflow of water. This exchange is necessary to support the various organisms living in the marsh."*

favorable conditions for plants called emergents. These plants can tolerate flooded soil and water depths to about twelve inches, but cannot be totally submerged for extended periods of time. Their roots are usually underwater, but leaves and stems are at least partially exposed to light and air. Plants typical of a shallow marsh include grasses, sedges, reeds, bulrushes, cattails, arrowheads, and pickerelweeds. Deep marshes contain floating plants, such as water lilies, bladderworts and pondweeds, as well as submerged plants, such as milfoils and coontails. Common plants found in wet meadows range from water-friendly grasses, sedges, and smartweeds to Joe-Pye weeds, swamp candles, blue flags, and touch-me-nots.

**Spotted Joe-Pye Weed (Eupatorium maculatum)** *Thick stands of dusty-rose wildflowers flourish in a wet meadow. A native perennial that can grow to over six feet tall, it is a good wetland indicator since it is seldom found in uplands. Native Americans and early pioneers used it as a medicine for numerous ailments.*

Now let's explore the intricate web of life revealed by the interplay of the myriad organisms that make up these ecosystems.

The path of life through a marsh begins with the energy of the sun as it illuminates the tiniest algae where photosynthesis takes place. The sunlight acts upon the water, carbon dioxide, and chlorophyll in the green plant, yielding water, oxygen, and carbohydrates (starches and sugars). This is a process we all learned about in school, yet somehow its profundity has escaped most of us. Photosynthesis is the only process on earth whereby living organic material can be created from sunlight. Most living things, except for some highly specialized bacteria and the communities of organisms they support, depend on the organic energy created by photosynthesis to live. Through the breath of plants, we all breathe and live. The very energy that fuels these thoughts is not separate from the health, vigor, and energy produced by the plant world.

Phytoplankton, consisting largely of algae and free-floating tiny plants and their remains, form the bottom of the food chain in the marsh. Zooplankton, composed of microscopic animals, their eggs and larvae, feed on phytoplankton, forming a second stage in the food-chain process. The zooplankton, in turn, are consumed by immature fish and the larvae of predatory insects. These then provide a food base for amphibians, reptiles, larger fish, and birds. Large mammals and humans constitute the top of the food chain.

In an inland-marsh ecosystem, the interrelationships among insects, plants, and animals are

**Fragrant Water Lilies (Nymphaea odorata)** *These beautiful plants often form a dense mat of platter-like leaves in marshes, ponds, lakes, and slow-moving streams. The undersurface of the leaves helps to create a microhabitat for a multitude of invertebrates, including insects, snails, and freshwater sponges.*

*ABOVE RIGHT:* **Common Cattail (Typha latifolia)**

abundant and easily observable. Reeds, bulrushes, and smartweeds provide excellent cover for nesting waterfowl, as well as for other birds and small mammals, such as the marsh rabbit. Red-winged blackbirds are often one of the first signs of spring in the Northeast as they return to the cattail marsh to establish territories and begin building nests of cattail leaves, sedges, and grasses found in the marsh. Aside from protection and nests, plants like smartweeds, sedges, bulrushes, and grasses produce seeds that are important food resources for waterfowl and other marsh birds. The tiniest duckweeds floating on the surface of a deep marsh are so named because of their significance as a food source for waterfowl. The larvae of damselflies, dragonflies, and mayflies supply protein to the young ducklings' diet. The roots or tubers of arrowheads, also known as duck potatoes, provide food for ducks and muskrats. Cattails, water lilies, pondweeds, and mussels are prime food items for muskrats, which also use cattails as construction material for their lodges and feeding huts.

These are but a few examples of the interdependency that exists in the freshwater marsh. From the tiniest plankton to the muskrat, each organism contributes to the richness of a vibrant ecosystem. Water, air, light, minerals, plants, insects, birds, mammals, and people are all intricately connected to form the whole. Changes to any part of the whole sends ripples through the entire ecosystem. The inland marsh is the wind sliding past a swooping northern harrier's wing, the song whistled by a young boy fishing, a wiggle in a bluegill being fed to a waiting otter pup.

**Old Stump, *Royalston, Massachusetts*** *Floating debris, stumps, and fallen trees are important parts of the marsh ecosystem. Though most of this tree is gone, the weathered roots at the edge of the marsh are beneficial as a platform for sunning turtles, or a perch for a feeding muskrat.*

*ABOVE LEFT:* **Bullfrog (Rana catesbeiana)**

Geographically, in terms of total area, the largest concentration of inland marshes is located in the prairie pothole region extending from the north-central United States into south-central Canada. It covers approximately 300,000 square miles, roughly one-third of which lies in the United States, mostly in North and South Dakota and Minnesota. This landscape is dotted with thousands of potholes — depressions formed by the action of glaciers during the Pleistocene era — which fill with snowmelt and rainwater in spring. Sizes of potholes range from quite small (the size of a living room) to the 10,000-acre Swan Lake in Minnesota, considered the largest prairie pothole in America. Most potholes are only a few feet deep, and vary in the types of vegetation that grow there, depending upon water depth, chemistry, and the length of the wet season. Some prairie potholes dry up in a matter of weeks or months, while others maintain water levels throughout the summer, except perhaps in years of extreme drought.

Whatever their individual size and composition, the prairie pothole region as a whole provides life support for millions of birds during annual migrations, as well as vital feeding and nesting areas for many species of waterfowl. In an average year, the pothole region is home to at least 50 percent of North America's waterfowl population. Most often surrounded by agricultural lands, potholes also function as natural water-treatment systems. They help collect and filter surface runoff, replenish aquifers and store floodwaters. Because of their rich soils and warm summer climates, these

**Rushes and Haystacks,** *Buchanan, North Dakota This prairie pothole, with its small pond and accompanying marsh, covers less than half an acre. Easily overwhelmed by the agricultural use of the landscape, many potholes have been lost through draining for cultivation. This pothole has been preserved, evidence of a growing breed of farmers who see beyond their immediate needs to embrace the importance of wetlands and the web of life.*

"*Unfortunately, like many other wetland habitats, prairie potholes have suffered major losses in acreage.*"

pothole marshes are considered to be among the richest in the world.

Unfortunately, like many other wetland habitats, prairie potholes have suffered major losses in acreage. One of the main contributing factors has been the extensive ditching and draining of potholes for cultivation, with often disastrous results. Draining the

potholes for increased farmland acreage may seem beneficial, but in so doing, the capacity of the land to hold water is severely reduced, creating a greater risk of flooding and crop damage. What happened at Lake Thompson marsh in South Dakota in 1985 is a striking example. Prior to that time, Lake Thompson was a shallow, 9,000-acre marsh. After heavy rains and snowfall,

**Scouring Rush and Prairie Pothole, *Manitoba, Canada*** *Scouring rush (Equisetum hyemale) create a marshy area in this Canadian prairie pothole. This native perennial plant and its relative, the common horsetail, are members of an ancient family of plants that grew to tree height in prehistoric times. They often form dense stands that help to anchor the soil.*

*ABOVE LEFT:* **Larger Blue Flags (Iris versicolor)**

the marsh swelled to become South Dakota's largest lake, inundating hundreds of thousands of acres, including roads and entire farms. Recommendations were then made to implement extensive restoration of these valuable pothole wetlands, particularly upstream in the watershed, so as to prevent future flooding.

As devastating as it was, this tragedy has resulted in a victory of sorts for wetlands. When it was determined to be too expensive to artificially lower the water table under Lake Thompson, the area became a project of the Prairie Pothole Joint Venture, part of the U.S.–Canadian efforts to preserve these threatened habitats. Similar projects are under way in other areas to preserve the remaining original potholes and to restore what's been lost. Since water does not recognize the political and economic boundaries we have established, it is absolutely necessary that private landowners, conservation groups, and state, provincial, federal, and international government agencies cooperate in these efforts.

The largest *single* marsh system in the United States, comprising approximately 7 million acres, is also perhaps the most well-known — the Everglades. Located in southern Florida, it is an exotic land of sprawling saw grass marshes and red mangrove swamps, extending from Lake Okeechobee southward to the southern tip of the state. A broad, flat, 50-mile-wide by 100-mile-long expanse that declines in elevation a mere two or three inches per mile, the flow of water is barely perceptible. It is easy to understand why the Everglades are often referred to as "the river of grass." This unique ecosystem supports many rare and threatened animals, including such diverse species as the Florida panther,

**Prairie Pothole, *Stutsman County, North Dakota*** *Depth of a pothole, length of the wet season, and water chemistry affect what types of plants will grow in the marsh. This can create distinct zones of vegetation, as evidenced by the ring of taller plants in this pothole nestled in the middle of grazing land. Small potholes may also contain populations of tiny crustaceans such as fairy shrimp and amphipods that serve as important food resources for migrating waterfowl.*

West Indian manatee, brown pelican, snail kite, wood stork, and American crocodile.

The Everglades provide us with an outstanding opportunity to examine some very important and far-reaching concepts that are crucial to an understanding of our place in the web of life. First is the realization that the only supply of water to the Everglades is rain. Before development of the Everglades, the rain fell on the earth, plants, and indigenous peoples. The water freely penetrated the ground and the aquifers filled. In the north, the Kissimmee River Basin swelled. Those waters flowed slowly south, filling Lake Okeechobee, the beginning of the 50 mile-wide river of grass. The water continued south, nourishing the whole of the Everglades, its creatures, peoples, swamps, marshes, and mangrove estuaries. All this happened in natural seasonal cycles.

The present-day scenario is quite different. It is estimated that more than half of the original Everglades has been drained, predominantly in the northern part, drastically altering the original ecosystem. (The more "natural" Everglades are preserved at their southern end in the 1.6 million acres of Everglades National Park.) Most of this alteration can be attributed to drainage and channeling for agriculture, as well as dams, dikes, and levees built to control floodwaters or to divert water supplies for farming, industrial, and residential use. In 1990, agricultural uses reached 3.8 billion gallons per day, while other human uses were at 14.1 billion gallons a day. The fact that Florida's population is increasing at 900 people a day, demanding 200,000 more

**Prairie Pothole, *McClean County, North Dakota*** *Formed in shallow depressions left by retreating glaciers some 12,000 years ago, these pockets of wetlands developed into thousands of marshes, ponds and lakes throughout the expansive plains area of south central Canada and north central United States.*

*ABOVE RIGHT:* **Sandhill Crane (*Grus canadensis*)**

gallons of fresh water daily, raises a very serious question of water shortages for the human population as well as the whole survival of the Everglades as we know it.

Now that the natural flow of water is completely controlled by levees, dams, and pumping stations, natural seasonal fluctuations are severely disrupted. The feeding and nesting patterns of wildlife, adapted to these natural fluctuations of alternately wet and dry seasons, are often disturbed by human manipulation of the water supply. Furthermore, rainwater falls on pavement or is gathered and hurried along in canals, no longer able to slowly filter through the earth into underground aquifers, an important source of pure well water. A coastal aquifer full of rainwater causes a positive pressure, which keeps seawater from entering. If an aquifer gets too low, salt water may enter it, destroying the water supply and inhibiting plant growth. Already an increasing number of people living on Florida's west coast are resorting to drinking desalinated water.

With the thirst of a growing human population, industry, and farming, the need for water is increasing. So who gets the water, the people or the Everglades? Unfortunately, like many controversial environmental topics today, the issue is framed as an either/or choice — people versus animals or people versus wetlands. However, there truly is no choice. To rob water from the Everglades to give it to people is to rob Peter to pay Paul. For the short term, people will have enough water, but to slowly drain the Everglades could have dire consequences for the future of Florida's aquifers and a continued supply of reasonably clean and salt-free water. A

vibrant Everglades, teeming with wildlife and the freely flowing water, *is* and sustains a healthy human community. The two are not separate. This is a point that can be made for most wetlands and their associated surroundings. There is no such thing as an endless supply of water. Human expansion must not exceed the supply of water. We must sustain all or eventually lose all.

Living in a world of cement slabs, computers, malls, and air-conditioned vehicles, many of us are unaware of wetlands, how they function, and the benefits they provide humankind. Though marshes sometimes provide ripe breeding habitats for mosquitoes, it is surprising to some people that mosquitoes are a vital link in the food chain: their larvae are an abundant source of protein for small fish, which in turn are fed upon by larger fish, all the way up the food chain.

Perhaps more directly related to humans and society, inland marshes play an important role in controlling rain, snowmelt, and floodwaters. Water can enter a marsh faster than it leaves. The plants of the marsh trap the water, slowing its movement, allowing for more evaporation and absorption by soil and plants. Filling in a marsh for development or draining it for agricultural land eliminates the natural function of the wetlands in providing important flood storage. As a result, many people have directly experienced the devastation caused by raging floodwaters. It has been found that the greatest flood damage occurs in areas where the highest percentage of wetlands has been destroyed. Eliminating wetlands further results in the need for

*ABOVE LEFT:* **Fragrant Water Lilies *(Nymphaea odorata)***

costly construction of dams and flood-control areas to replace lost flood-storage capacity. Studies have shown that, for the most part, these artificial methods do not do nearly as good a job as the original, natural wetlands.

There is another important benefit of a marsh. When water is slowed by a marsh, some sediments or toxic materials have time to settle out, which can result in 90 percent cleaner water downstream. Large amounts of nitrogen and phosphorus entering a marsh are also trapped and taken up by plants and soils during the spring and summer, again resulting in cleaner downstream waters. This in turn means cleaner streams, aquifers, and reservoirs for drinking-water supplies, fishing, and recreation.

Inland marshes may also moderate local climates. The pavement of a city street radiates the heat of the summer sun, compounded by vehicle exhaust systems adding carbon to an already uncomfortable situation. Over by the marsh, however, plants are producing oxygen, while evaporation from water and from plant leaves (evapotranspiration) adds moisture to the air, and the openness of the marsh allows for circulation. The water of the marsh also acts to absorb heat by day and slowly releases it by night when the temperature is cooler.

Some scientists believe that inland marshes and other wetlands are important factors in the world's available nitrogen balance. With the increased burning of fossil fuels, sulfur in the atmosphere (sulfates) is also greatly increased. These sulfates are washed out of the atmosphere in the form of acid rain, which is killing many of our ponds and lakes, especially in the

**Saw Grass Prairie, Everglades National Park, Florida** *Saw grass (Cladium jamaicencis) is a member of the sedge family and covers nearly 8 million acres of the Everglades open prairie. Indigenous Native Americans called these areas Pa-hay-okee, meaning grassy waters. Dwarf cypress, a stunted form of pond cypress, often grow scattered throughout the saw grass prairies.*

Northeast. Marshes, however, can trap and remove some of these sulfates, preventing them from returning to the atmosphere.

Many people have experienced the strong smell emitted in a marsh when the mucky black bottom is disturbed. This is a mixture of hydrogen sulfide and methane. There is some evidence that methane plays a role in the viability of the ozone layer in the upper atmosphere, which shields us from excess ultraviolet radiation.

Inland marshes produce hay and other foods for livestock and wild rice for human consumption. Some plants used by ducks and muskrats are also edible for humans, providing not only food, but enjoyment and satisfaction for the forager willing to gather them. Such wild-food possibilities include the well-known cattails, but also roots of tuberous water lilies, spatterdocks, and arrowheads. It is important to remember, however, that over-harvesting and grazing in marshes have had serious adverse effects, and any use of these fragile wetlands must be approached in a sensitive manner in order to protect and preserve the integrity of the ecosystem.

The effects of an inland marsh reach far beyond its physical boundaries. Inland marshes support upland wildlife and deepwater fisheries, directly and indirectly providing opportunities for hunting and fishing. The economic benefits are reflected in the fact that three-quarters of America's fisheries depend on inland and coastal wetlands for their existence. This multibillion dollar industry provides more than 1.5 million jobs.

(The economic value of California wetlands alone has been estimated at $10 billion per year.)

Inland marshes have an aesthetic appeal as well. Many artists and photographers are drawn to favorite wetlands, which elicit their deepest sense of creativity. One may even catch a glimpse of a wildlife photographer's floating blind moving slowly along the margins of the marsh. Bird-watchers know that inland marshes provide them with some of their most exciting hours in the field. Whether one is looking for the opportunity for casual nature study or in-depth scientific research, inland marshes are fertile havens.

Our own experience bears this out. On an excursion to a local New England marsh to photograph young great blue herons in the adjacent beaver pond, we were treated to an unexpected visitor. We were sitting quietly, camouflaged behind the tall grasses and reeds along the marsh edge, when, quite suddenly, we heard loud, boisterous splashing in the open water just beyond our view. After several minutes, the mystery creature left the water and headed our way. Perfectly still and nearly breathless, we waited as the tops of the grasses swayed, then parted — to reveal the glimmering, water-streaked fur of a river otter twelve feet away. It bounded out of sight after several excited moments, to continue its pursuits along the edge of the marsh. It returned to inspect us several times until eventually it ventured within seven feet. For a moment we were convinced it was going to nuzzle our boots. But caution seemed to prevail over curiosity: the river otter, its nose perpetually in the air, savored one last sniff of these two

*ABOVE LEFT:* **Swamp Milkweed (Asclepias incarnata)**

strange creatures reclining at the marsh edge before continuing on its way.

Wildlife experiences enrich our lives and are an added benefit to be found in marsh habitats. There is, however, something far more important than all the benefits we list here. It is the awareness of the funda-mental reality that we are not separate from the marsh. By describing all the benefits marshes provide for us, we continue the illusion of separateness. If we per-ceived ourselves and the marsh as one entity, a unified whole, we would not need to substantiate all the reasons why it's important to preserve and protect them.

**Tussock Sedge (Carex stricta)** *This is one of the more easily recognizable plants in the hard-to-identify sedge family. Aptly named because of its habit of growing in dense clumps (tussocks) in freshwater marshes as well as wet meadows and swamps, it is a native perennial with grass-like leaves two to three feet high. Its roots, called rhizomes, help to anchor soil and prevent erosion during flooding.*

# COASTAL

# WETLANDS

*In wildness is the*

*preservation of the world.*

- Henry David Thoreau

aking our living in the world of nature photography certainly has its rewards. A trip along the Maine coast is a case in point. The land is replete with riches, from the swaying grasses of the tidal marshes to the steep, treacherous, and rugged coastline. Here where earth meets sea, an interface of two worlds occurs, each giving life to the other, each defining the other. To stand on the edge of these two worlds is to be sometimes overwhelmed by the sights, sounds, and smells of earth, water, and sky, as they coalesce into one enormous feast for the senses. Here one glimpses the powers of creation and receives, if attentive, an inkling of the mysteries of life. There is a palpable rhythm, constant yet ever changing, moving in and out, like a heart beating, though so slowly at times as to be almost imperceptible.

Before we begin to define coastal wetlands, it is important to understand that ocean, continent, and wetlands are all intimately connected in one large ecosystem. Although we find it necessary to label and distinguish them in order to talk about them, we feel it is far more crucial to understand that the fundamental reality is their interconnection and oneness. An example of this interrelationship on a smaller scale is the tidal marsh-barrier beach association. A barrier beach is a narrow strip of beach and dunes that protects the tidal marsh from the wave action of the open sea. Although the dunes and sands above the tidal zone are considered uplands by some definitions, their existence *is* the

**Barrier Beach, *Crane Reservation, Ipswich, Massachusetts***
*Here extensive dunes provide quieter waters on the bay side allowing for the development of salt marshes. Dunes are an integral part of the existence of the salt marsh ecosystem.*

OVERLEAF: **Predawn at Sandy Neck, *Cape Cod, Massachusetts***
*Beneath a sandy beach lies a world of creatures. Sanderlings, a starling-sized bird that ranges worldwide, are a common site scurrying along the water's edge in search of tiny crustaceans and mollusks exposed by retreating waves.*

existence of the tidal marsh wetland. Without this buffer, the tidal marsh would not exist. Tidal marsh and barrier beach must be seen as one interconnected ecosystem.

Coastal wetlands are highly diverse in appearance, character, and composition, from mud flats and sandy beaches to estuaries and salt marshes to tidal pools and rocky shores. One common factor is that they are primarily driven or sustained by the ebb and flow of oceanic tides. For our definition, coastal wetlands are bounded on the land side by the extreme high water of monthly spring tides and on the ocean side by the outer edge of the continental shelf. On the East Coast, the continental shelf is usually a gentle slope that extends downward before dropping off into the depths of the ocean, whereas on the West Coast the drop is steeper and more dramatic.

Let's take a closer look at the types of coastal wetlands, beginning with the tidal marshes. Three main types of tidal marshes are discussed in this chapter: salt marshes, brackish marshes, and tidal freshwater marshes. In North America, tidal marshes are most prevalent along the East Coast, the Gulf Coast of the United States, the southern shoreline of Hudson Bay in Canada, and the coast of Alaska. With a few exceptions tidal marshes on the West Coast are much less developed due in part to the steep topography of the land. In southern Florida, coastal marshes give way to subtropical mangrove swamps; these are indeed coastal wetlands, but we have chosen to cover them in the chapter on Swamps.

**Rocky Shoreline, *New England Coast*** *Winter snow, wind, and waves buffet these rocks. A few of the life-forms that can adapt to the harsh conditions of the splash zone are yellow and gray lichens. Only a few terrestrial animals, such as mites, spiders, and ants, feed in this zone.*

One of the most important requirements for the development of a tidal marsh is that it be protected from the constant wave action of the open sea. Therefore, they are usually found behind barrier islands, sand spits, in sheltered bays, and on protected coastal plains, as well as near the mouths of rivers. Some well-known examples include the salt marshes behind the Outer Banks along the Carolina and Georgia coasts, Chesapeake Bay, the Bay of Fundy, Suisun marsh near San Francisco Bay (the largest estuarine marsh system in the the contiguous United States, and the extensive marshes in the Mississippi Delta and the Gulf Coast of Louisiana.

Fluctuations in the amount of salt, the time submerged and open to the air, the type of sediments, and temperature variations each play an important role in determining the type of tidal marsh that will develop and be sustained in a particular environment. It is important to remember that these ecosystems exist as a continuum and do not always fit into the strict boundaries we assign them by definition.

Tidal marshes are some of the most productive ecosystems in the world, rivaling the tropical rain forests. Some coastal marshes are capable of producing up to 27.5 tons of vegetation per 2.5 acres a year. Nearest the

**Salt Marsh at Low Tide, *North Atlantic Coast*** *The grasses in this salt marsh have a bronzed appearance due to the effects of weathering and the rich colors of the rising sun. Salt and brackish marshes serve as important nursery shallows for flounder, bluefish, menhaden, and many small fish that later move into deeper waters.*

ocean and most affected by the tides are the salt marshes. Scientists distinguish two distinct zones here, the lower (intertidal) marsh and upper (high) marsh. The low marsh is closest to the saltwater source and is normally flooded and exposed daily. It may be laced with tidal creeks, and is predominantly covered by a single plant species: the tall form of smooth cordgrass *(Spartina alterniflora)* on the Atlantic and Gulf coasts, and California cordgrass *(Spartina foliosa)* on the West Coast. The upper marsh (closer to the uplands) is flooded irregularly, sometimes only monthly during spring and storm tides. Exposure to the air is of longer duration. The vegetation here is more diverse, including the short form of smooth cordgrass, salt hay or salt meadow grass *(Spartina patens)*, spike grass *(Distichlis spicata)*, and black grass *(Juncus gerardi)*. The latter is replaced in southern marshes by another rush species, *Juncus roemerianus.*

Salt marshes can be harsh environments for vegetation, but a closer look at the salt marsh grasses reveals some interesting adaptations. To survive the high salinity of the salt marsh, cordgrass has salt glands that can secrete excess salt, which is visible as salt crystals on its leaves. Furthermore, though its roots are deep in mud with little available oxygen, its stems have hollow tubes that

**Salt Marsh in Winter, *Gloucester, Massachusetts*** *Salt marsh grasses grow on mud flats at the mouth of this small creek as it enters the Atlantic Ocean. Salt marshes tend to form in areas that are protected from waves, such as behind barrier beaches or sheltered bays. This salt marsh is quite small, and may not have the necessary requirements to expand or maintain its size.*

*ABOVE RIGHT:* **White Ibis *(Eudocimus albus)***

transport oxygen from the leaves to the roots, providing the necessary air for survival.

Historically, cordgrass provided thatching material for early settlers' roofs and salt hay grass was used as fodder and the marsh as pasture land for livestock. Today these grassy marshes continue to buffer stormy seas and are able to absorb heavy metals, such as mercury, lead, iron, copper, and other pollutants, before they reach the sea. Perhaps the most important role for marsh grasses is their extensive contribution to the biomass of the marsh as a whole, as well as their contribution to the food chain in particular. When the marsh grasses die, they are decomposed by bacteria, breaking the plants down, forming detritus (dead organic matter), so that they can be taken up by plankton, which in turn are fed upon by clams, crabs, shrimp fry (baby fish), and other animals. These plants also provide food for deer, muskrats, and geese, as well as ducks, rails, and other birds. They also offer shelter and nesting sites for many species of migrating waterfowl, as well as lodging material for muskrats.

The next time you sit down to a meal of clams, crabs, shrimp, or flounder, think for a moment about what you are eating — and about the act of consumption itself. The food before you has weight and substance. Flounder, for example, consume small crustaceans, shrimp, mollusks, and worms. These invertebrates in turn are largely dependent upon nutrients from the tidal marsh, in the form of detritus and plankton. These microscopic plants and animals are part of your own consumption. As you bite into the flounder, 10,000

**Salt Marsh, Jacob's Point, Warren, Rhode Island** *The formation of "cowlicks" is typical of salt marshes composed primarily of salt meadow grass. Some salt marshes slowly gain elevation each year from a combination of decomposing grasses and sediments brought in with the tides.*

*ABOVE LEFT:* **Roseate Spoonbill** *(Ajaia ajaja)*

beings have also taken a bite, from the tiniest bacteria on up. Yet most consumption is done totally oblivious to this whole process, oblivious to the contributions of 10,000 beings.

Moving inland along a coastal river, immediately upstream from the salt marshes, we find the second type of tidal marshes: the brackish marshes. Here fresh water mixes with salt water in greater quantities. Brackish marshes are mostly associated with estuaries, which are transitional zones where rivers and streams meet the ocean. Brackish marshes are thus influenced by both river and ocean, fresh and salt water. Chesapeake Bay in eastern Maryland and Virginia is the largest estuary in the United States, with many rivers draining into it. At the estuary, the incoming seawater brings its loads of beneficial nutrients to the marsh. When the tide ebbs, or recedes, it removes debris and particulates. The receding ocean water is immediately followed by the fresh water of the river, which enriches the marsh with organic material, minerals and silt.

Species diversity in these brackish marshes is limited by the ability of different life-forms to adapt to the fluctuations in daily temperature, salinity, and alternate drying and submergence. Nevertheless, this maze of tidal creeks, fish, nutrients, plankton, and fluctuating water levels forms a dynamic ecosystem, which supports spawning, feeding, and nesting opportunities for many fish, avian, and mammal species. The extra-high levels of beneficial nutrients support dense populations of

**Salt Marsh, *Tiverton, Rhode Island*** *Smooth cordgrass is the dominant plant in this salt marsh, which is flooded by tides at least once a day. There are two forms of smooth cordgrass, a tall form up to six feet, and a shorter form usually less than eighteen inches. They spread by underground rhizomes, building a strong underground network.*

mollusks, crustaceans, shellfish, diatoms, and millions of fry. In fact, approximately two-thirds of the major commercial fish species are dependent upon estuaries and salt marshes for their existence, whether directly as feeding areas for adults or as nurseries for fry and juveniles. Anadromous fish, those that migrate from the sea to fresh water to spawn, may travel through estuaries on their way upstream, and juveniles often linger in estuaries prior to their return to the ocean. The most well-known anadromous fish is salmon, but alewife, smelts, shad, and striped bass make a similar journey. In Washington's Puget Sound, juvenile salmon feed mainly

**Salt Marsh after a Long Winter, *Maine Coast*** *This photo shows a variety of habitats that typically appear along the Northeast coast: freshwater creeks enter the ocean and may deposit enough silt to create elevated substrates upon which salt marshes can grow. Rockweeds and periwinkles are scattered among the rocks. The farthest rocks, separated from the mainland at high tide, are off limits due to their use by nesting shorebird colonies.*

*ABOVE RIGHT:* **Snowy Egret (*Egretta thula*)**

on the larvae of salt-marsh midges, which subsist on detritus. Two-thirds of East Coast shellfish and crustaceans, such as clams, oysters, crabs, and shrimp, spend their lives as free-swimming larvae in tidal marshes.

Vegetation in the tidal brackish marsh is varied, mostly as a result of fluctuations in salinity. Along the south Atlantic and Gulf coasts, black needlerush is the dominant plant in the brackish marsh closest to the salt marsh. In northern areas, salt-hay grass, narrow-leaved cattail, bulrushes, and reeds (phragmites) are common. As one moves farther upstream, the variety of vegetation increases as fresh water further dilutes the salinity level. Pickerelweed, wild rice, arrowheads, smartweeds, sedges, and a host of other freshwater-tolerant plants begin to appear. Salt marsh species gradually give way to tidal freshwater species.

Further upriver from brackish marshes but still close enough to the ocean to be affected by tides, we find the third type of coastal marshes: the tidal freshwater marshes. Usually these form where the topography is flat, the tide range is significant, and there is enough rainfall or river flow to support a freshwater environment. They are most predominant on the Atlantic coast from New Jersey to Georgia. There are also extensive tidal freshwater marshes on the Gulf Coast, but these are affected more by wind tides than by lunar tides. In either case, as the tide starts to enter the salt marsh, the river backs up and begins to swell beyond the reaches of brackish water and into the tidal freshwater marsh. Here the water is slowed, allowing nutrients to drop out and

**Morning Light, Cobscook Bay State Park, Maine** *Low tide along the Maine coast exposes different zones in this coastal wetland. At the lower end of the slope closest to the ocean, rockweeds almost completely cover the rocks. Closer to land, salt marsh grasses glow golden-red with the first rays of the morning sun.*

enrich the tidal freshwater marsh. These marshes very closely resemble inland freshwater marshes; they will often blend together and are hard to distinguish.

Tidal freshwater marshes receive a lot of the same beneficial inputs as the brackish and salt marshes, that is, a heavy nutrient exchange due to the constant inflow and outflow of water. In addition, the tidal freshwater marsh doesn't receive the stress of saline water, which limits species diversity. Tidal freshwater marshes have many of the same values and ecology as the inland freshwater marshes covered in the first chapter, with the added benefit of extra nutrients due to tidal conditions.

Another type of coastal wetland associated with estuaries is the mud flat. Mud flats form where the shoreline is sheltered from severe waves and currents, that is, protected bays, gulfs, or estuaries, and behind barrier beaches, where the slope is gentle and where there is enough sediment to accumulate. This occurs when the water moves very slowly over the land, allowing the minute suspended particles of sand and mud to drop out and build up. Tidal marshes sometimes form on the higher elevations of mud flats where the slope is shallow enough for salt marsh grasses to grow, and barrier beaches often protect both from erosion.

For anyone who lives near the coast or has the opportunity to visit it, there's nothing quite like the experience of exploring mud flats at low tide. The truly primeval feeling of bare feet in oozing mud connects us in a very visceral way to this magnificent world. As children, we remember being spellbound by the air bubbles we encountered as we walked along, the telltale clue to

the presence of unseen lives under the surface. To many people, however, mud flats look like a vast, uninhabited wasteland. This is quite far from reality, for mud flats are teeming with life, from the tiniest microorganisms to progressively larger and more recognizable animals. Bacteria, diatoms, and blue-green algae live in the top half inch of the mud, where light and oxygen are sufficient for their survival. A bit larger in size are a variety of species of nematodes, very slender, primitive worms that can achieve astonishing densities. Other worms include thread worms, mud worms, and blood worms, the last of which can grow to eleven inches long and are a prized bait for fishermen.

Perhaps the more familiar residents of the mud flats are the many varieties of shellfish and crustaceans that thrive there. Several species of clams, oysters, mussels, and crabs inhabit these intertidal flats. Oysters can form extensive beds and are commercially harvested in such areas as Chesapeake Bay on the Atlantic Coast, Willapa Bay on the Pacific Coast, and on Louisiana's Gulf Coast. Numerous species of fish feed on mud flats when the rising tides allow it. One resident, the fiddler crab, is best known for its unique mating behavior. The male crab stands in front of its burrow (either in the mud flats or in the banks of a tidal creek in the salt marsh) and waves its one enlarged claw to attract females and ward off competing males.

This abundance of food also attracts many bird species to the mud flats as well as to the neighboring marshes. Beyond the ubiquitous gulls, many species of wading birds, including herons, egrets, sandpipers, and

**Mud Flats and Tidal Marsh, *Willapa Bay, Washington*** *This pristine estuary is home to plants and animals that depend upon the delicate balance of the estuary for their survival. Flooded irregularly, the top layer of sediments dries out when exposed, creating a jigsaw-like maze. A close look reveals the tracks of a river otter most likely searching the area for a meal of crab or waterfowl.*
*ABOVE LEFT:* **Tri-colored Heron (Egretta tricolor)**

yellow legs, forage for food here. The mud flats also serve as significant "staging" areas for migratory shorebirds all along the Eastern seaboard. Many species use these areas to store up necessary protein for their long spring and fall migrations. An occasional otter, mink, or raccoon will also frequent these areas. The most well-known reptile of the salt marsh and mud flats is the diamond-backed terrapin, capable of crunching up crustaceans and mollusks in its jaws. Unfortunately, this once-common turtle has been greatly reduced in numbers by being overharvested for its prized meat.

We have talked about coastal marshes and mud flats with their diverse array of plant, microbe, and animal interactions. We turn now to another coastal wetland, the tidal zone associated with the rocky shore of ledges, cliffs, and boulders. These rocky shores are particularly abundant along the Northeast coastline from New England to Canada and on the West Coast from California to Alaska. Life clings in many forms to the rock-hard substrates exposed sometimes to pounding surf and relentless tidal currents. Here, too, as with the estuary, the incoming tide brings with it a multitude of microbes and plankton, which become food for life clinging to the rocks. The receding tide carries with it wastes and the beginning of new life in the form of eggs and larvae.

Scientists distinguish several levels or zones in this ecosystem, with slight variations between East and West coast tidal zones. Beginning closest to land is the splash or spray zone, the area above the high-water mark where salt spray reaches. Here colonies of lichen sometimes decorate the rocks with bright orange patches. Just below this is the black zone, so called because the minute blue-green algae that colonize this area often appear as a black slime on the rocks. These algae are among some of the oldest and most primitive living things on earth. Next is the periwinkle domain, though these marine snails will move up into the black zone to graze on the algae there. Below the periwinkles, exposed to the most severe pounding waves, winds, and extreme changes in temperature, live the barnacles in what is called the high intertidal zone. (Intertidal areas are those that are alternately exposed and submerged by daily tides.) Barnacles can get such a tenacious grip on the rocks, it is as if they have become part of the rocks themselves. Here among the barnacles, periwinkle larvae may settle and grow, but as they mature, the periwinkles must move up or away from the constant action of the surf to more protected areas for a better footing. Barnacles feed on minute planktonic organisms by filtering them out from incoming tidal waters. They in turn are subject to predation by dog whelks, a carnivorous snail.

Moving toward the ocean into the mid-intertidal zone is the rockweed zone. Rockweed, sometimes called sea wrack, is a brownish, rubbery-looking seaweed with little bulbous air sacs that sometimes pop when stepped on. These are really air bladders, which help buoy the rockweed at high tide. Rockweed often grows in thick clusters and provides a haven for periwinkles, crabs, snails, worms, and other small creatures that need shelter, especially at low tide. Below the rockweed is the low

*ABOVE LEFT:* **Harbor Seals (*Phoco vitulina*)**

intertidal zone, in which we find red-brown Irish moss and sea lettuce. Below this and beyond the tidal zone lie brown kelp, which is rarely uncovered by the sea. Along the Pacific Coast these ribbons can sometimes exceed 100 feet in length. Highly nutritious and quite tasty, seaweeds are harvested on both coasts, and are a healthy addition to one's diet — as long as they are gathered from unpolluted waters. Sea urchins, crabs, starfish, sponges, anemones, sea cucumbers, worms, and jellyfish are also likely inhabitants of these lower zones.

Amid the nooks and crannies of these rocky shores, often unnoticed and passed by, are the jewels of

**Tidal Zones, *Seal Rock State Park, Oregon*** *The tall haystack rocks in the distance show distinct bands of color depicting different zones of life in the rocky shore habitat. The black in the spray zone is a covering of lichens, analogous to the brightly colored lichens in the spray zone of the North Atlantic coast. The band of white represents thousands of barnacles, which also cling tenaciously to the rock surfaces in the foreground.*

the seashore: the tide pools. These enchanting habitats are formed in little catch basins when the tide recedes, leaving them full of seawater and with many of the life-forms mentioned above. These pools usually contain very clear water, allowing easy observation. They are a definite "must-explore" for anyone with a little time to spend and the curiosity and eagerness to observe nature up close. They can vary greatly in plant and animal activity, depending on geography and location within the tidal zone. In the mid and lower tidal zone pools, one might encounter anything from snails, periwinkles, crabs, anemones, barnacles, starfish, and blue mussels to rockweed and Irish moss. Raccoons, otters, mink, and many birds also visit these rich pools of life, seeking a meal. The higher tide pools, filled by splashing waves and/or rain water, may contain green maidenhair algae, small crustaceans, mosquito larvae, flatworms, and microscopic animals.

Coastal wetlands are profoundly diverse and complex, an intricate interweaving of innumerable life-forms. As wondrous as they are, they continue to be in jeopardy on many different levels. Numerous small impacts can often add up, causing long-term problems. According to census information as of July 1991, 54 percent of the U.S. population lives in coastal counties on the Atlantic, Pacific, and Gulf Coasts and on the shores of the Great Lakes. Pressure to fill in coastal wetlands for development, and pollution of coastal waters, particularly near major metropolitan areas, remain serious threats to the health and continued existence of these wetlands.

Alaska's southern coastal wetlands are at particular risk due to the "1 percent rule," which allows the state to destroy up to 1 percent of its wetlands. This would have a devastating effect on critical fisheries' habitat, impacting the economic stability of the state. Most states in the contiguous U.S. have enacted special laws to protect coastal wetlands, but vigilance must be maintained to see that protective measures are enforced and encouraged.

The first step in saving coastal wetlands (and wetlands in general) is to understand their wholeness and dispel the notion of a world of separate things. For a moment, imagine yourself in a tidal marsh: the winds have abated, revealing a deep and timeless calm. The marsh is rich with the dance of life and death. It is as though the pulse of creation is most powerful here. Yesterday, today, and tomorrow, coastal marshes touch all our lives. It is imperative that we develop a world view where protecting and sustaining oneself means protecting and sustaining the whole. We need to more clearly understand that it is not possible to comprehend one single blade of marsh grass, one microbe, the flight of a shore bird, or the light that silently illuminates the marsh without fully embracing the whole. The very light that shines on the marsh and is absorbed by the leaves is being prepared to light our own minds. When we understand this connection — this vast web whose threads reach out to connect us all in this great mystery we call life — when we cease to fragment life, we do not need to be convinced to save the marsh. Then our dance, our celebration, *is* the dance of the fiddler crab and the graceful steps of the heron feeding in the marsh.

**Tidal Pool and Rockweeds, *Rhode Island Coast*** *This tidal pool is surrounded by rockweeds, and upon close inspection, periwinkles are visible, feeding along the bottom. These watery worlds are fascinating spots for nature observation.*

*ABOVE RIGHT:* **Rockweeds (Ascophyllum nodosum and Fucus vesiculosus)**

# PEATLANDS:

# BOGS & FENS

*Let us give Nature a chance;*

*she knows her business*

*better than we do.*

Montaigne

In North America, most people will get to visit a wetland at some point in their lives. More than likely, the type of wetland they encounter will be either a river, stream, pond, lake, or seashore. Less frequent are the opportunities for explorations deep into the reaches of a boreal bog or a walk on a floating mat of vegetation. One must remember to tread carefully here, as there are many types of rare plants and much of this ecosystem is fragile and easily disturbed. It's also possible to sink out of sight and not be seen for 2,000 years or so.

Due to the highly acidic conditions, low oxygen levels, and slow decomposition rate found in bogs, remarkably preserved bodies thousands of years old have been discovered and pondered over by scientists and anthropologists through the ages. Danish author Peter Glob has written about the preserved remains of people from the Iron and Bronze Ages in his fascinating book, *The Bog People* (Cornell University Press, 1969). In the whole of Europe, more than 1,500 bog people have been found, from different cultures and centuries. Some of them date as far back as 3,500 years ago. It is theorized that bogs were of great importance to the Germanic cultures of northern Europe, and for some of these people, bogs were highly spiritual places. It is suggested that certain bogs were believed to be sacred to the gods.

**Floating Fen, Harvard Pond, Petersham, Massachusetts**
*Exploring these floating mats of vegetation can be challenging because of the fragility of the environment as well as the uncertainty of the mat's ability to support weight. A closer examination of the yellow flowering plants on these floating mats reveals a colony of horned bladderworts (Utricularia cornuta) in full bloom.*

*OVERLEAF:* **Ponemah Bog, New Hampshire** *The formation of this bog in a glacial kettle hole began around four to six thousand years ago. Little by little the floating mat of vegetation has spread over the surface of the pond, with the accumulated peat underneath steadily filling in the lake. This three-acre pond is all that remains of the original 100-acre lake.*

Sacrifices were made to Nerthus (Mother Earth), the goddess of fertility. Besides human bodies, which showed evidence of violent death, many objects were believed to have been left in bogs as offerings. Cauldrons, trumpets, thousands of swords, spearheads, arrowheads, and shields have been found in northern Europe.

One might ask, what was it about these bogs that made them sacred to these ancient earth-based people? We may never have an unequivocal answer to this question, but the spirit of their mysterious and otherworldly ambiance remains with us today. For us, time spent in bogs has been quiet, soothing, and meditative. There is an intangible quality to these wetlands that pulls one down to the earth. Perhaps it's the often

**Peatlands, Ontario, Canada** *A small area of sphagnum moss almost submerged by water is surrounded by a larger expanse of sedges that eventually give way to a black spruce bog in the background. In Canada peatlands are most commonly referred to as muskegs.*

*ABOVE LEFT:* **Rose Pogonias (Pogonia ophioglossoides)**

dominant sphagnum mosses with their visually sensuous texture: soft, moist, and inviting. Underfoot, it feels more luxurious than the most exquisite carpeting, even surreal in some way, a bit luminous, ancient, and healing. It also seems to absorb sound, adding to the tranquil essence of the bog.

We've encountered some of the more mysterious elements of bogs as well. One such experience occurred on a trip to Peacham Bog in Vermont, one of the largest quaking bogs in New England. The section we were exploring was fairly open in spots, dotted with black spruce and tamarack trees, and very dense in others, with peatlands covered in sphagnum moss and, in some places, waist-high shrubs. It was a very calm, sunny late-summer day, a little hot, without a breeze. We had drifted apart, each examining different plant communities. We were careful not to shout to each other because, as with certain places in nature, there was a special quality we wished not to disturb by talking. Into this silence there unexpectedly arose a subtle sense of a presence, as though an invisible entity had walked into the open. We felt we were looking directly at it but couldn't see it. Eventually we heard the sound of something slicing quickly through the shrubbery. As the sound intensified, we noticed a small black spruce tree being whipped back and forth by a forceful, swirling wind. Most people would have called it a small "twister" or a "dust devil," though it was quite ghostly with neither color nor shape, and was visible only by the effects it produced in the surrounding vegetation. After making a few passes within our line of sight, it simply vanished. Where did it come from, and how did it happen on such a calm day? It certainly added mystery and wonder to the bog for us.

There is often some confusion with terms when people speak of bogs, so let's examine more closely what we

**Pitcher Plants (Sarracenia purpurea)** *Deep red, nodding flowers grow on separate stalks from the pitcher-like leaves from which this carnivorous plant derives its name. Nine species of the pitcher plant family are found in North America: one in the Pacific Northwest, one north of Virginia in the East, and the remaining seven in the Southwest.*

mean when discussing these wetlands. The title of this chapter includes three terms: peatlands, bogs, and fens. Of the three, "peatlands" is the broadest in scope and includes bogs and fens. Peatlands exist in many parts of the world, in diverse climates, and at various altitudes. In this book, we deal mainly with northern peatlands, the most extensive type in North America. The Okefenokee Swamp, parts of the Everglades, and the "pocosins" of the mid-Atlantic coastal plain also have underlying peat substrates, but are discussed in other chapters because they better represent other types of wetland communities. It should be noted that peatlands are often referred to by different names in different parts of the world: a heath in Maine, a muskeg in Canada, mire and moor in Europe, to cite a few. The one ingredient all peatlands share is water. There must be a surplus of water that is impeded in some way so that it does not drain off quickly. The decomposition of organic matter (dead plants and animals) must be slower than the production of matter in order for peat to accumulate. In other words, the top layer of vegetation keeps growing faster than the underneath layers decompose. One reason for this is that matter decays much more slowly in water than when it is exposed to air. The partially decomposed organic materials build up and form peat. Lands covered with peat are called peatlands, analogous to lands covered with trees being called forestlands.

Northern or boreal peatlands are most widespread in Canada and Alaska; Canada has the highest concentration of peatlands in the world at over 600,000 square miles. The lower United States also contains

**Meddybemps Heath, _Meddybemps, Maine_** _Lying in the distance, sparsely dotted with white pine and spruce, Meddybemps Bog is a national natural landmark of approximately 2,000 acres. A complex system, it contains a variety of habitats including sphagnum mats, leatherleaf and other shrub-dominated areas, and small pools._

these boreal wetlands, with most occurring in the north-eastern and Great Lakes regions of the country, especially northern Minnesota and Maine. There are smaller pockets in the Pacific Northwest, the western mountains, and the Appalachian Mountains in West Virginia.

What type of peatland will develop in a given area depends on several factors. Peatlands form where there is high moisture and the water level is above or just below ground level. Aside from the amount of water that is present, acidity, oxygen and nutrients are also significant players.

There are different types of bogs, but in its strictest sense, the term "bog" connotes a type of peatland that has no nutrient import or export except for

**Leatherleaf Bog, *The Pine Barrens, New Jersey*** *Located in southern New Jersey, this bog is typical of peatlands located in this coastal plain habitat. Often forming adjacent to streams or springs in old ponds, they can also be found in cut-over white cedar swamps (dead trees in background) and abandoned cranberry bogs, and are sometimes referred to as "spongs".*

***ABOVE LEFT:*** **Bull Moose *(Alces alces)***

rainwater. In other words, a bog is a nutrient-poor, isolated wetland with peat as the substrate. It receives moisture mainly through precipitation, is low in minerals, high in acidity, and low in plant diversity. Sphagnum mosses are the dominant species that decompose to form peat. The water is usually cold, stagnant, and low in oxygen. This definition best describes a raised bog.

Here peat deposits accumulate to such an extent that they fill the original glacial basin and grow above and beyond groundwater levels. They are referred to as ombrotrophic (meaning "rain-fed") peatlands, and these are the most acidic and poorest in nutrients. There are also level bogs, which develop in glacial kettle holes or lakes and are relatively small (usually under

**Wild Cranberries (Vaccinium macrocarpon)** *Native large cranberry seen here growing wild, is one of the original species first harvested from bogs in the New World. Commercial varieties of cranberries are grown in bogs in southeastern Massachusetts, New Jersey and Wisconsin. In many cases, the creation of artificial bogs for commercial cranberry production has led to a significant loss of natural wetlands in these areas.*

200 acres). With little inflow or outflow of water, they are also acidic and low in nutrients. The floating or quaking bog we visited in Vermont is an example of a level bog. These quaking bogs (so called because the surface "quakes" when walked upon) are basically floating mats of vegetation that initially develop along the shore of a pond or lake, then grow from the shoreline out over the water. They may spread over the entire area or leave a much-diminished opening in the original pond. Eventually the peat grows thick enough to support a person's weight, but care should still be taken when exploring them. It is still possible to fall through, and it's much more difficult getting out than falling in. Level bogs are often covered with sphagnum mosses, leatherleaf, and sheep laurel, as well as cranberries, cotton grass, sweet gale, pitcher plants, and black spruce and tamarack trees.

One other type of bog is called a blanket bog. These are located along maritime coasts, especially in Newfoundland and Labrador in the east, and Alaska and British Columbia in the west. Similar blanket bogs are found in Ireland and Scotland. They require cool-temperature coasts with lots of moisture and fog. They literally "blanket" the land features, covering ridges, valleys, and slopes alike, sometimes sprawling over vast areas quite removed from the initial spot where the peat first originated.

Fens, on the other hand, are peatlands that have a nutrient import and export. Water and nutrient sources are derived from surface and groundwater as well as from precipitation. Though it may be nearly

**Atlantic White Cedar Bog, *Cape Cod National Seashore, Massachusetts*** *Atlantic white cedar (Chamaecyparis thyoides) also known as southern white cedar, is an aromatic evergreen tree that ranges from central Maine to northern Florida, but is primarily a southern coastal plain species with only scattered locations remaining in New England.*

imperceptible, water flows through a fen, carrying with it some mineral soils. This results in a higher level of available minerals, greater plant diversity, and less acidity, creating a more fertile peatland. Sedges and woody plants are often the principal peat sources in fens. Fens are often subdivided into two categories: rich and poor fens. Rich fens are those described above, where the water has moved through mineral soil, thereby increasing the level of nutrients in the fen. Rich fens are minerotrophic (meaning "mineral-nourished") peatlands. Poor fens are considered to fall between bogs and rich fens. In some cases, a forested or shrub-covered bog or peatland may be called a swamp, or a poor fen. Some scientists consider poor fens to be a transitional stage toward bogs. In the other direction, rich fens may grade into marshes. These gradations and transition zones sometimes make precise definitions difficult.

Now that we've described different types of peatlands, let's take a closer look at what actually makes the peat. Most often the dominant plant component is this marvelous "stuff" called sphagnum moss, also known as peat moss. There are well over 250 species worldwide. Each species has its own requirements for water, pH, and sunlight, allowing for adaptations to different growing conditions. Only the very upper layers of this plant grow, while the lower layers die off and form peat. This plant is remarkable in its ability to hold water, up to twenty times its own weight. For this reason, in its dried form, it was commonly used by some Native Americans as a diaper material that was stuffed into babies' cradle-boards to absorb moisture. Dried sphagnum moss has also been used to stuff pillows. Because of its acidic quality, which inhibits bacterial growth, it was used for surgical dressings during the First World War. We've experienced the effects of sphagnum moss after applying it to a rash acquired on a hike. There was a slight burning sensation at first, but after an hour or so, the condition improved greatly. Sphagnum is capable of locking up large amounts of carbon before it can get into the atmosphere, which can help to mitigate the greenhouse effect. It also acts as a sink for some heavy metals, retaining them and preventing them from dispersing.

Peatlands do not support as large a variety of wildlife species as do some other types of wetlands, but they are home to some extraordinary and uniquely adapted plants, which add a touch of the exotic to this ecosystem. Many of the plants, including the sphagnum mosses, have developed different strategies to survive in this nutrient-poor habitat where most other plants would be unable to live.

One specialized group of plants utilizes insects and small animals to obtain the necessary nutrients that most plants would pick up with their roots. These are called carnivorous plants. The Venus flytrap of the southeastern U.S. is what probably comes to mind when most people think of an insect-eating plant, but the carnivorous plants of peatlands do not snap shut on their prey. Pitcher plants, sundews, and bladderworts have all developed their own entrapment methods to attain the food they need. The pitcher plant is the largest of the three. As its name implies, it is shaped like a pitcher to

**New England Floating Bog** *Early morning ground fog partially shrouds this floating bog. Bogs have traditionally been places of great mystery and mysticism, from the Iron Age to the present. Bog explorations have turned up preserved bodies and scores of treasures hundreds of years old, believed to be offerings to the gods.*

hold water and special digestive juices. The plant has developed colorful veins as well as scent to attract its quarry. Once an insect enters the vessel of the plant, tiny hairs, which point down, make it harder for the insect or other small organism to escape. The prey eventually ends up in the liquid collected in the bottom of the "pitcher" and dies there, often by drowning. The enzymes, helped by normal decomposition, slowly work to extract nutrients from the organism, which are then utilized by the plant.

Sundews, on the other hand, have a clear, sticky liquid on glandular hairs attached to their leaves. Once an organism is trapped by these sticky hairs, the hairs and leaves fold inward very slowly toward the prey, which is then digested and absorbed. Over 25 percent of

this plant's nitrogen can be secured from the body parts of insects.

Aquatic bladderworts have evolved a different system of obtaining food. These plants are without roots, but have deflated sacs along their underwater leaves. When the sacs are stimulated by tiny organisms, they inflate and suck the animal into the bladder through a small orifice. Once inside, special enzymes go to work to digest the captured prey.

Carnivorous plants are but a few of the many plants that grow in peatlands. Over 150 different species of sedges are adapted to life in peatlands, most of which will be found in fens. For the novice, these species can be hard to identify and distinguish one from the other. Cotton grass, however (which is a sedge and not a grass),

**Cedar Needles and Sphagnum Moss** *Northern white cedar (Thuja occidentalis) needles rest upon a mat of sphagnum mosses. Primary peat producers in many nutrient-poor bogs, sphagnum mosses reproduce both vegetatively and through the dispersal of spores. A close look at this photo shows small, red-brown spherical spore cases on thin stems at the top of some branch tips.*

can be identified very easily when in bloom, even at a distance, by its tufts of what looks like white cotton. There are several species that grow from nine to forty inches high, and they have a wide geographical range. We have encountered cotton grass from Alaska to Oregon to the state of Maine and within a fifteen minute drive of our home in Massachusetts. It can also be found as far south as Kentucky and Florida, and in northern Canada as well. Cotton grass has the ability to preserve nutrients by transporting them away from leaves to underground organs. Cotton grass fruits, a brown triangular seed, are eaten by mallard ducks before the leaves fall at the end of the growing season. Other animals, such as voles, beaver, and deer, may also make light use of this plant.

Bogs and fens, especially the latter, are often the best habitats to observe some of the world's most exquisite plants: members of the orchid family. Of the estimated 15,000 to 30,000 species of orchids worldwide, there are around 200 species found in North America. Some of the more familiar orchids found in peatlands include rose pogonia, grass pink, swamp pink, bog rein orchid, and bog twayblade, though in some areas these will be quite uncommon. There are also some very rare species. The small white lady's slipper, which seems to prefer calcareous (calcium-rich) fens, is on the federal list of threatened species. In the boreal peatlands of the North, Ram's-head lady's slipper is quite rare throughout its range. Others species, like calypso, are restricted to areas where northern white cedar grows.

Not all peatlands are composed of the vegetation we have mentioned thus far. Shrubs may also be the dominant plant species or intermix with the sphagnum mosses and sedges. Typical woody shrubs include leatherleaf, Labrador tea, and bog rosemary, all of which are evergreens, as well as diverse species of blueberry, cranberry, and laurel. One of our most memorable wild food foraging treats were the native blueberries and cranberries we picked in a few isolated bogs while on a shoot deep in a maritime forest on Cape Cod, Massachusetts. The hike was hot and strenuous, but the blueberries were so cool, sweet, and wet! We marveled at the variety of flavors, each species with a unique taste of its own.

Aside from supplying us with trailside nibbles and berries that find their way into many delicious and creative recipes, shrub bogs provide important cover and some food resources for wildlife. Snowshoe hare can be found here seeking protection in winter and browsing on blueberry twigs. Blueberries are important to a wide range of wildlife, from white-footed mice and chipmunks to black bear, songbirds, and grouse. It may come as a surprise to many people, but foxes, coyotes, pine martens, and fishers are also very fond of this fruit, and will eat it in large quantities. White-tailed deer browse blueberry twigs and, in Minnesota, leatherleaf and Labrador tea as well. In some locations, moose have also been known to eat Labrador tea. Cranberries are used on a limited basis by sharp-tailed grouse and Hudsonian godwit.

Peatlands are not only covered by shrubs, sedges, and sphagnum mosses, but also by certain trees.

*ABOVE RIGHT:* **Round-leaved Sundew (Drosera rotundifolia)**

Black spruce, tamarack, Atlantic cedar, and northern white cedar are the most common species. The black spruce is especially adapted to a wet habitat. As sphagnum builds or as water levels rise, the spruce tree establishes higher roots. Tamaracks, sometimes called larches or hackmatacks, resemble evergreens in that their leaves are needles, but unlike spruce and other conifers, they shed their needles each fall like other deciduous trees.

In winter, these forested wetlands provide exceptionally good cover for mammals and birds, as well as provide roosting and nesting sites in other seasons. White-tailed deer browse extensively on cedar twigs and foliage. The seeds of black spruce cones are well used by red squirrels and other small rodents. In some areas, porcupine, white-tailed deer and hare will eat the twigs and foliage. Spruce grouse, ruffed grouse, and blue grouse eat the needles. Tamarack needles and buds are used by grouse, while crossbills and red squirrels feed on the seeds.

Through the centuries, peatlands have served humankind in a variety of ways. Past and present uses include mining for fuel to fire electrical plants, to warm homes and for insulation. Bog iron, a low-grade form of iron ore that develops in peat deposits, was mined in the United States and elsewhere in the eighteenth and nineteenth centuries. Many people are familiar with the use of peat moss as a soil supplement in the garden and as a potting medium to start seeds because of its ability to aerate, fertilize, and hold water. Native cranberries and blue-

**Rose Pogonias (Pogonia ophioglossoides)** *Bogs and fens provide the necessary soil conditions and cool temperatures that many orchid species require. Rose pogonias often prefer open to semi-open sphagnum/sedge mats, and sometimes grow in the same areas as other orchids like grass pink (Calopogon tuberosus) and dragon's mouth (Arethusa bulbosa).*

*"Bogs and fens are often the best habitats to observe some of the world's most exquisite plants: members of the orchid family."*

berries are common crops from peatlands, as are different kinds of forest products, such as black spruce and cedar. Peatlands are even being used in some countries for sewage treatment because of their ability to remove phosphorus and nitrogen through natural processes. Perhaps one of the more benign uses of bogs is the extraction of samples in order to examine its historical archives. Within the sometimes more than forty feet of accumulated peat are records frozen in time. Pollen records, dust, soil, volcanic ash, radioactive and magnetic particles, seeds, leaves, bones, and even heavy metals are preserved and recorded here. A treasure of information awaits scientists who are becoming more and more proficient in reading this data. Already the historical information gathered from these vaults, dating as far back as 10,000 years, shows a disturbing trend in the upper layers of the peat. In examinations of the last forty years of peat, studies have documented the accumulation of new substances: heavy metals, radioactive fallout, PCBs, DDT, and other possible contaminants and health hazards. This is clear evidence that humans are rapidly changing the environment. We know very well that we can only change an ecosystem so much before that change will make it impossible for certain species, and ultimately the integrity of the whole system, to continue. Already the changes humans have brought to this world have caused the extinction of thousands of species. As we continue to mine and drain these bogs, converting them to crops, fuel, and fertilizer, we must ask always if what we are doing is truly necessary, and whether there are less harmful or destructive alternatives than these current practices.

There are only a limited number of peatlands. What we use can't be replaced easily, as it takes from 5,000 to 10,000 years for them to form. With so many demands upon their utilitarian attributes, peatlands could easily be used up, right out of existence, if we do not take care to preserve and protect them now.

**Cotton Grass, *Talkeetna Mountains, Alaska*** *Cotton grass, a member of the sedge family with grass-like leaves and cottony flower heads, grows in wet peaty soils, often in shallow water. There are many species of cotton grass in the northern areas of the continent (fourteen in Alaska alone). It is often found covering large areas of the tundra.*

*ABOVE RIGHT:* **Cotton Grass (*Eriophorum spp.*)**

It is easy to see that peatlands are unique ecosystems with a full complement of animal-plant-people interconnections. Peatlands are very much a feature, a part of the whole, of who we are. To eliminate them would be to change a component in the matrix that is the human species. It is not important to protect peatlands just because they have a certain aesthetic appeal or because we can fire electrical generators with them, but because they are part of what constitutes the entirety of the natural world. To recklessly destroy different aspects of the natural world could eventually spell doom for our own species. We protect these wetlands not just for their own sake, but for our sake as well, out of intelligence and respect for who we are and for future generations. This is not an environmental attitude that cares more about animals or plants than it does about people. It is an environmentalism that truly cares about the whole of the human race and its continuance. It reflects an intelligence that is not self-centered and is not overly concerned with immediate financial and material gains. To act with future generations in mind is not to forfeit anything, but to fulfill a greater meaning and perception of who we are.

Charles W. Johnson, in his book *Bogs of the Northeast* (University Press of New England, 1985) eloquently summarizes the reasons why peatlands are worthy of preservation:

> Though we have come a long way in gaining knowledge of peatlands, we still do not know enough to answer all the important questions that have been asked. Maybe we don't even know all the questions that should be asked. But at least we do know that peatlands are not just strange blotches on the landscape, nor useless, nor unimportant. Rather, they store treasures of our natural heritage and provide refuge for rare species of our earth. Where abundant, they can give us fuels and products we seek in this demanding age. They can be magical inspirations for the minds and souls of people. And they, like tall mountains above, broad seas beyond, or nestling forests that surround, should claim some autonomous recognition, apart from our personal or selfish judgments — for simply being here, with us, on earth together.

**Spruce Bog, Baxter State Park, Maine** *This bog is densely forested with lichen-covered black spruce (Picea mariana) and carpeted with sphagnum mosses. Small pockets of sheep laurel (Kalmia angustifolia) add a touch of diversity. Northern peatlands are generally located in areas where temperatures are cool and high humidity causes excessive moisture to accumulate.*

*ABOVE RIGHT:* **Highbush Blueberry (Vaccinium corymbosum)**

# SWAMPS

*We are rooted to the air*

*through our lungs*

*and to the soil*

*through our stomachs.*

*We are walking trees*

*and floating plants.*

- John Burroughs

Swamps evoke unpleasant, maybe frightening, images for many people. Portrayed as vile and nasty environments in literature and film, it's no wonder they have come to epitomize no-man's-land. The plots of late-night movies with titles like *Creature from the Black Lagoon* or *The Swamp Thing* were invariably similar: a dark and slimy creature would surreptitiously emerge from some ominous swamp to terrify unsuspecting victims. Fed a diet of fear of the unknown, it's often a big step for some people to appreciate the fascinating world of swamps. For those who venture into these habitats, however, a world of mystery and enchantment reveals itself in surprising and often exquisite shapes, sights, and sounds.

The word "swamp" is often used very loosely to describe any waterlogged piece of land. Whether bog, marsh, or wet woodland, to most people it's simply a swamp. For our purposes, the term "swamp" denotes any tree- or shrub-covered wetland or floodplain of either fresh or salt water. There are so many different types of tree- and shrub-covered wetlands in North America that it is impossible to discuss all of them in depth here. Some of the more significant include the cypress, tupelo, and mangrove swamps in the southern portions of the United States; the bottomland

**Bald Cypress and Duckweeds, *Merchants Millpond State Park, North Carolina*** *A lush green carpet of duckweeds covers the dark reflective waters of this bald cypress swamp. These tiny floating plants provide food and cover for many of the swamp's inhabitants. Bald cypress are among the largest and oldest trees in the southern U.S. Some are estimated to be over 2,000 years old.*

***OVERLEAF: Bayou de View, Brinkley, Arkansas*** *Coffee-colored water surrounds these water tupelo (Nyssa aquatica) trees in early spring. These alluvial river swamps are usually continuously flooded and form in depressions on the floodplain, such as in sloughs or old river channels, and are sometimes referred to as backswamps. The color of the water is caused by an abundance of tiny suspended particles of sand, silt, and clay.*

(floodplain) swamps of the Mississippi Valley; the pocosins most dominant in the Carolinas; and red maple swamps. (Red maples are the most geographically widespread trees in the eastern half of the U.S., and although these trees grow in uplands, they often form extensive stands in wetlands.) To the north and into Canada we find black spruce, tamarack, and cedar swamps, most of which are forested peatlands.

Some of our favorite places to visit are bald cypress swamps. The trees themselves are magnificent, sometimes towering giants with bulging, awesome buttresses (adaptations to high water levels). In the Black River area of North Carolina are ancient bald cypress trees believed to be over 2,000 years old. To place yourself amongst these giants — with hanging Spanish moss overhead, green duckweed floating upon the dark waters, and cypress "knees" (cone-shaped structures) protruding from the thick black muck—is to be transported into another world. Some of these swamps can be truly transcendent.

Cypress trees are conifers, but like tamaracks, they are deciduous, meaning they lose their needles in winter. There are two types of cypress, bald cypress (*Taxodium distichum*) and pond cypress (*Taxodium ascendens* or *Taxodium distichum var. nutans*). Bald cypress swamps are found along the Atlantic coastal plain from southern New Jersey to southern Florida, then west along the Gulf Coast through southern and western parts of Alabama, most of Louisiana and Mississippi, and into Texas. Northward they extend into southern and eastern Arkansas and follow the Mississippi

**Red Maple Swamp, *Millers River, Royalston, Massachusetts*** *Unlike the water-loving cypress and tupelo trees of southern swamps, red maple swamps develop in poorly-drained depressions that are only periodically flooded, and where soils remain too saturated for upland species to grow. They often form in lowlands adjacent to rivers and streams.*

*"Bald cypress can achieve heights of 150 feet
and may live more than 2,000 years."*

floodplain north to the southernmost parts of Illinois and Indiana. Bald cypress can achieve heights of 150 feet and may live more than 2,000 years. Normally, however, big trees are more likely to be from 105 to 120 feet tall and two to four feet around, though some trees can reach ten feet in diameter. The wood is highly resistant to decay and for this reason is especially prized for lumber and used for shingles, docks, and bridges, among other things. Water tupelo (*Nyssa aquatica)* may be found growing alongside bald cypress. When we use the term "cypress swamps," it does not necessarily exclude the presence of tupelo or black gum (*Nyssa sylvatica*), or other plant species.

Bald cypress swamps may grow along the banks

**Bald Cypress Trees, *Seashore State Park, Virginia*** *The trunks of these bald cypress exhibit enlarged, swollen bases referred to as "buttresses," believed to be due to their growing in flooded conditions. The trunks and branches of the trees are often festooned with the wispy gray leaves of Spanish moss, one of the classic epiphytic plants associated with southern swamps.*

***ABOVE RIGHT:*** **Larger Purple Fringed Orchis (*Platanthera grandiflora*)**

of rivers, where there is likely to be a nutrient-rich environment. Depressions running along the river, but often separated from it at low water, are also ideal for the growth of bald cypress and water tupelo. These depressions are intermittently flooded by high water, which bathes the swamp with a fresh supply of nutrients needed by the bald cypress. Bald cypress and water tupelo also grow along lake edges. Seasonal fluctuations of water levels and rainwater runoff from uplands supply the necessary nutrients.

Pond cypress is considered a subspecies of bald cypress by some scientists and a different species altogether by others (hence its two Latin names). Geographically not as widespread as bald cypress, it is found primarily in southern Georgia and Florida, and to a lesser extent in southern Louisiana, Mississippi, and Alabama, and along the coastal plain in the Carolinas and southern Virginia. Pond cypress wood is said to be of the same quality as bald cypress, though it usually doesn't grow as large. It is more adapted to nutrient-poor sites than is bald cypress and can be found at higher elevations. Unlike bald cypress, which often grows with water tupelo, pond cypress is more often associated with black gum. Both types of cypress trees live in almost permanently flooded conditions and cannot tolerate brackish water.

One of the more interesting land features associated with cypress trees are structures called cypress domes. Looking at them from a distance, as we have across saw grass marshes in the Everglades and wetland prairies in the Okefenokee Swamp, cypress domes look

**Merchants Millpond State Park, North Carolina** *Bald cypress and water tupelo grow together in this swamp. Each of these species grows in pure stands in the southeastern U.S., though it is thought that pure water tupelo stands result from selective logging of bald cypress.*

*ABOVE RIGHT:* **Black-Crowned Night-Heron (Nycticorax nycticorax)**

like hills, but in actuality they are depressions in the landscape with cypress growing in them. The taller trees grow in the middle and the shorter ones off to the edges, so the crowns of the trees form a domed shape. Beneath these domes are usually impermeable or mostly impermeable substrates, which allow for the retention of water. These domes or cypress ponds are nutrient-poor compared to riverbanks and lakeshores, conditions more suitable for pond cypress than bald cypress. Pine, sweet bay, and swamp red bay may also grow in with the pond cypress.

When growing under very poor nutrient conditions, pond cypress growth may be stunted and the trees scattered. These areas are often referred to as pygmy

**Cypress "Knees", Seashore State Park, Virginia** *These strange, conical-shaped projections lend an otherworldly atmosphere to this virgin forest of bald cypress trees. These adaptations to the roots are thought to result from the almost permanently flooded condition of the swamp. Initially believed to function as anchoring systems for the trees in deep water, scientists are also examining the possibility of their function in the tree's respiratory system.*

*ABOVE LEFT:* **American Alligator (Alligator mississippiensis)**

cypress or dwarf cypress swamps. Dwarf cypress are typically ten feet high and do not usually reach more than twenty three feet. Because of their suppressed growth, some of these trees are actually much older than they appear. They are a common sight scattered in the saw grass marshes of the Everglades and in Big Cypress National Preserve.

One of the most enchanting aspects of cypress swamps immediately draws attention to itself upon entry. Whether it's the first visit or the hundredth, one can't help but notice the cone-shaped objects protruding from the dark, reflective water and wonder what they are and what their function is. These cone-shaped structures, called cypress "knees," are adaptations of the cypress roots. Pond cypress, tupelo, and black gum also produce types of knees, but none compare with the number and size of those produced by the bald cypress. We have observed cypress knees that measured over five feet high, and although most were typically less than four feet, there are recorded heights of over twelve feet. Scientists have long debated the significance of these adaptations. Some argue that knees help stabilize or anchor the trees into the muck of the swamp, while others claim that this root adaptation is a way to help a waterlogged tree breathe. Despite research efforts, the function of cypress knees still remains unclear.

Other attention-grabbers in cypress swamps are often not the trees themselves but the fascinating epiphytes, or air plants, that grow on the trees and in the canopy. Contrary to what many people believe, epiphytes are not parasitic plants. Although they do attach themselves to trees, they do no measurable harm to their host. Air plants produce and acquire their own food from air, dust, and rainwater.

The best-known air plant, Spanish moss, is not a moss at all but belongs to the pineapple family, the bromeliads. Its long, silver-gray threadlike leaves drape loosely over the branches in swaying bearded tufts. Other bromeliads include stiff-leaved wild pine, ball-moss, twisted air plant, and many others.

The swamps also play host to many beautiful and even some famous epiphytic orchids. Unfortunately, many species have been overcollected. Habitat loss and poaching by commercial and amateur collectors have been responsible for a dramatic decline and, in some cases, the extirpation of some of these orchids. The epidendrum and the cowhorn orchids are two of the more popular orchids, the former for its beauty and the latter for its size: some specimens weigh as much as seventy five pounds.

Imagine for a moment a plant growing from a small seed to seventy five pounds of air, dust, and water. It boggles the mind to think of a single plant collecting all that mass. Now widen the view and think of the entire cypress swamp, its biomass and productivity. There is a tremendous process occurring here, this accumulation of living matter. What we are really talking about is air, light, water, and earth. It always amazed us, growing up near farms, to watch the silos fill with corn and the barn fill to overflowing with bales of hay. Where did all this matter come from? Nothing but air, light, water, and earth. We are prompted to ask what

*ABOVE RIGHT:* **Tickseed and Cypress Needles**

then is the biomass of people on this planet, and what is the substance of all that matter? Are we much different than the frugal air plant or the ancient cypress? It seems evident that we are all kin— beings of air, light, water, and earth.

The understory plants (the lower vegetation that grows beneath the trees) of cypress swamps are very diverse and depend on the type of swamp, climate, hydrology, geography, and the amount of light. There may be a dominance of woody plants or herbaceous plants or a mixture of both. Some swamps with high water levels have little or no understory, but might have prolific mats of duckweed floating on the surface.

The productivity of cypress swamps—their ability to generate different life-forms — is dependent on hydrology, or water cycles, and the availability of nutrients. The most productive of the cypress swamps are the cypress/tupelo swamps that are neither too wet nor too dry, but receive seasonal pulses of alluvial (detrital material deposited by running water) flooding. When these same ecosystems are impounded, their productivity is lowered. Receiving less nutrient input, lake- and river-edge bald cypress swamps are also not as productive as the backwater swamps receiving seasonal impulses of nutrient-loaded waters. This inflow of detritus forms the bottom of the food chain in the swamp. Invertebrates, such as midges and amphipods, are highly dependent on detritus, some directly and some indirectly, and they in turn are valuable food for fish. Other invertebrates in these wetlands are freshwater shrimp, snails, worms, crayfish, clams, and the larvae of insects.

**Pond Cypress Swamp, *Okefenokee National Wildlife Refuge, Georgia*** *Pond cypress swamps are more limited in their geographical range than are bald cypress. They are found primarily in Florida and southern Georgia and tend to grow in areas that are poor in nutrients, and less subject to the effects of river flooding. In Big Cypress Swamp and in parts of the Everglades where pond cypress grow stunted and scattered in the marshes, these wetlands are referred to as dwarf cypress swamps.*

Different fish use cypress swamps for spawning, feeding, and cover. Deep in the swamps, or when the swamp is temporarily cut off from a fresh supply of water, oxygen levels can be low, making it difficult for certain species of fish to thrive. Bowfin and gar, two primitive species that have remained relatively unchanged for millions of years, and some types of minnows, have adapted to living in these oxygen-poor conditions.

Reptiles and amphibians are abundant in the southern cypress swamps. The most famous of the reptiles is the alligator. The American alligator can grow to over seventeen feet long and is the largest reptile in North America. During the drier winter season, alligators excavate holes, aptly called "gator holes," which provide a cool, watery environment for themselves as well as other wildlife. The watering hole provides a sanctuary for many species that would not survive without it, but it also works as the alligator's bait, luring animals from afar to its little oasis in a world that is slowly drying up. Juvenile alligators dine on insects, crayfish, snakes, and frogs, while adults also eat small fish, mammals, birds, and turtles. Alligators are not restricted to swamp habitats; they are also quite at home in the wetland prairies of the Okefenokee and the saw grass marshes and river sloughs of the Everglades.

The endangered American crocodile also inhabits swamps, but its range is limited to southern Florida and it frequents more coastal areas than the alligator. The crocodile looks similar, but has a narrower snout and is lighter in color than the alligator. Its fourth tooth is visible when the jaw is closed, distinguishing it further from its look-alike.

Southern cypress swamps are productive and diverse ecosystems. Merchants Millpond State Park (2,918 acres) in North Carolina is one of the most fascinating places we have visited. Exploring the park by canoe, one enters a world of cypress, water tupelo, hanging Spanish moss, and mistletoe. Below swim many different species of fish, including the long-nosed gar and the bowfin mentioned previously. Over 190 species of birds have been recorded in the park. The Francis Beidler Forest, a National Audubon Society Wildlife Sanctuary lying in the Four Holes Swamp near Harleyville, South Carolina, is another stunning example of the diversity of species found in these environments. At the heart of this 6,000-acre sanctuary is the biggest old-growth stand of bald cypress and tupelo in the world. The ecosystem supports 40 species of amphibians and 50 species of reptiles, as well as 44 species of mammals, 39 species of fish and 140 species of birds.

No discussion of swamps would be complete without including the mangroves. Although they are tree-covered coastal wetlands and could be considered under either category —swamps or coastal wetlands— we have chosen to cover them here with other swamps. Mangrove swamps are found in tropical and subtropical regions throughout the world. Here in North America, they range from Florida along the Gulf Coast to Texas. Mangroves are evergreens and can be killed by frost,

which limits their northward expansion. Florida's southwest coast supports one of the largest mangrove swamps in the world.

Throughout the world over sixty species of mangrove exist, but there are only three that grow in the southern United States. Red mangrove is easily recognized by its arching roots and grows well out into the mud flats. Black mangrove tends to grow a bit more inland, in areas where it may be covered at high tide but exposed at low tide. Black mangroves have root projections called pneumatophores, small cigar-shaped objects that protrude from the water, possibly similar in function to cypress knees. Red and black mangrove often mingle. The third type is white mangrove: this tree usually grows even farther inland, and has no outstanding root structures. In some locations all three mangrove species may be found growing together.

Mangroves can live in salt water or fresh water, but they do not compete well with other freshwater plants. However, they do gain an advantage when salt water enters the picture. A large portion of mangrove wetlands exist in estuaries, where fresh water meets salt water. These estuarine mangrove swamps are constantly replenished with nutrients transported by fresh water from the land and flushed by the ebb and flow of tides. The mangroves' decomposing leaves contribute to the nutrient level with loads of detritus, which supports a bursting population of bacteria and other decomposers, sustaining billions of nematodes, protozoa, and other small organisms. These in turn feed fish and shrimp, right on up the food chain to wading

**Mangrove Swamp, *Everglades*, *Florida*** *Red mangroves are the predominant species in this coastal swamp in Everglades National Park. Their arching prop roots secure them to the ground and, along with interlacing branches, form a dense maze. The cigar-like shapes protruding from the water are the specialized root structures of black mangroves.*

birds, pelicans, the endangered crocodile, and people.

Brackish mangrove swamps are particularly valuable as nurseries for shrimp and recreational fisheries. In Florida, these resources support a multimillion dollar business. If the nutrient load that sustains these fisheries was lost, this industry would be doomed along with it, as would a whole way of life for many people. At some distance away, over 100 miles in some places, lies a grave threat. The waters that traditionally flowed from the Kissimmee River to Lake Okeechobee, formed a river of grass 50 miles wide as it continued southeast and west through saw grass and cypress swamp to the estuary where it deposited its life-giving load of nutrients. These waters have been and continue to be

**Red Mangroves, *Everglades, Florida*** *Red mangroves dot this spike rush marsh at the limit of their inland expansion in the southern coastal section of the Everglades. In the background, tree islands, referred to as hammocks, often form on slightly elevated ground throughout the Everglades*

dammed, leveed and canalled for development, industry, and agriculture. As water throughout the Everglades is diverted from its natural course, less of it winds its way to the estuary. The water is literally being turned off. This is significant because the whole expanse of the estuary is controlled by the amount of fresh water flowing into the coastal area. During the summer rains, the zone of brackish water expands seaward. In the winter dry period, the brackish zone narrows. The disruption of these natural rhythms is destructive: too much or too little water entering the estuary can have a devastating effect on its species composition and productivity.

Bottomland or floodplain forests are another type of wooded wetland. These are sometimes referred to as "riparian wetlands," meaning relating to the bank of a stream or river. In the West, they are sometimes called "bosque" or "stream bank vegetation" and in the central and eastern United States as "bottomland" and "floodplain forests". For our purposes here, we use these terms interchangeably.

Floodplain forests can be found where streams or rivers periodically overflow their banks. The highest concentration of bottomland forests are in the Mississippi River Valley, reaching up into southern Illinois. Other major sections are in the Southeast where rivers and streams flow into the Gulf and Atlantic Coasts. These riparian ecosystems can spread over several miles wide in these areas, whereas in the arid West, riparian forests usually form narrow strips along stream and riverbanks.

Floodplain forests are located between two ecosystems, upland on one side and a river or stream on the other. These areas are especially high in productivity and species diversity for plants and animals because of the deposition of rich alluvial soil from floods. These wetland forests are noted for growing beautiful trees as well as for providing significant wildlife habitats. Since a large number of upland creatures feed in this rich wetland area, these animals transport much of the energy of the aquatic food chain to upland communities, making the uplands more valuable as well. Many of these fertile forests have been drained and cleared for agriculture and other purposes, contributing to the loss of over 70 percent of riparian wetlands in the United States.

In examining tidal marshes, mangrove swamps, and other wetlands, we have noted the significance of the import and export of detritus and other nutrients to the productivity of ecosystems. The hydrologic action of tides and fresh water from a river meeting in an estuary—the pulsing and flushing as if inhaling and exhaling—results in the marsh and mangroves receiving nourishment and giving nourishment to the surrounding environment. The floodplain forest also receives the benefits of extra nourishment from floodwaters, which make detritus, clays, minerals, and other important nutrients available. These riparian wetlands are intermittently flooded, determining, along with soils, the types of trees able to grow there. During periods of flooding, the vegetation must be able to tolerate a lack of oxygen at the roots. However, since flooding is not

permanent, aeration does occur, enabling more vigorous growth than could be found under permanently flooded conditions. It's like having the best of two worlds: the incoming nutrients brought by floodwaters and the availability of oxygen during dry periods. Depending upon topography, these riparian forests may receive nourishment not only from floodwaters, but also from the adjacent uplands during rain. Furthermore, while they receive all this nourishment, they also contribute by producing tons of organic material, mainly through the decomposition of leaf and plant litter. The floodwaters bring nutrients and minerals, but at times, they also pick up and carry away large amounts of detritus, feeding it to freshwater marshes and the organisms that live there at the bottom of the food chain. The journey continues to the estuary, to the brackish tidal marsh and to the mangroves. When you hear the sound of a great blue heron or an osprey circling smoothly above, you have heard a leaf drop in the forest and the murmur of a brook speaking of life.

The value and importance of riparian forests extends beyond this export of nutrients: they can also act as sinks that trap pollutants, providing for cleaner water downstream. In fact, some studies show that certain bottomland forests can transform inorganic forms of nutrients to organic forms. This seems to indicate that the bottomland forest has again enriched the waters flowing to the estuary.

The forested floodplain is so diverse in plant species that a complete list is too lengthy to include here. One partial list for the southeastern bottomland

**Bald Cypress Swamp, *St. Francis National Forest, Arkansas***
*Dark lines on the trunks of these bald cypress (Taxodium distichum) trees reflect the high-water mark of flooding in this bottomland forest adjacent to the St. Francis River, near its confluence with the Mississippi River.*

***ABOVE LEFT:*** **Duckweed and Pondweeds**

forests contained 75 different species of trees and shrubs alone. This diversity, plus the positioning between uplands and a waterway, make these riparian ecosystems especially valuable to wildlife, benefiting land as well as aquatic species. Because of the elongated shape of many of these wetlands, they also serve as crucial wildlife corridors. Studies have shown that there is more wildlife activity in floodplain forests than in the adjacent upland forests. The importance of this ecosystem to wildlife cannot be overemphasized. Whether utilized for breeding, nesting, feeding, commuting, or for cover, the riparian forest provides an "oasis" for wildlife. Like the tidal zone, this ecosystem is an interface of two worlds, a crossroads of diversity and abundance.

**Bottomland Hardwood Forest, *Beall Woods State Park, Illinois*** *This floodplain forest at the confluence of Coffee Creek and the Wabash River is inundated by spring floodwaters. These forests are most often associated with rivers and streams, and serve a vital function in the slowing, absorbing, and storing of floodwaters. They once covered vast areas of the Mississippi River Valley floodplain, but most have been cut down for their valuable timber and cleared for agriculture.*

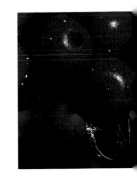

Along with the tree-dominated swamps discussed thus far are certain shrubs adapted to growing in different wetland conditions. Leatherleaf and Labrador tea are able to grow in nutrient-poor and acidic conditions. Other common shrub types that may form in large concentrations are alder, willow, and buttonbush. The alders (related to the birches, ironwood, hornbeam, and hazelnuts) are widespread in North America. They can at times form dense, impenetrable stands. They are good buffers against erosion, and provide excellent animal cover. Ptarmigan and grouse feed on buds, while hare, beaver, deer, and moose feed on the twigs and foliage of these shrubs. Alders, like legumes, are nitrogen fixers, adding valuable nitrogen to the soil, which aids plant growth.

Pocosins are an important shrub wetland found on the eastern coastal plain from Virginia to northern Florida. The word "pocosin" is an Algonquin word meaning "swamp on a hill," referring to the fact that these shrubs grow on elevated spots in association with different waterways. Pocosins have been referred to as evergreen shrub bogs because they are found growing on and producing peat. Pocosins are commonly dominated by red bay, loblolly bay, sweet bay, and pond pine, and smaller woody plants, such as fetterbush, titi, and wax myrtle. The value of pocosins is similar to that of the riparian forests. They act as a buffer against flooding, as a sink for pollutants, as feeding, nesting, resting, and migratory corridors for wildlife. They also have a relationship to the estuary, by supplying nutrients to it and trapping agricultural runoff before it reaches the estuary.

Throughout history, people have often viewed swamps as not only frightening, but problematic in a practical sense: they couldn't be farmed, logged, or navigated easily. In addition they bred all those horrible mosquitoes, water moccasins, and alligators. It was believed that all kinds of predators hid out in those foreboding swamps, with a few hermits, weirdos, and outlaws thrown in for good measure. With this type of attitude, it's not surprising that "Drain it!" was the persistent cry.

The need to conquer fear was reflected in the need to conquer nature. A dynamic was established whereby "man against nature" was the primary interaction. This is evidenced in phrases like "to eke out a living with one's own bare hands," connoting that one needed to fight, conquer, and control nature in order to get something from it. Thus a battle cry arose against many of the continent's great swamps, and man declared war on them. Attempts to drain the Great Dismal Swamp, located in southeastern Virginia and northeastern North Carolina, began as early as 1763, with George Washington among those who led the charge. (A 5-mile ditch in the Great Dismal Swamp National Wildlife Refuge still bears his name today.) In the years that followed, along with a 22-mile long canal, 140 miles of logging roads were constructed. Ancient cypress, some possibly over 2,000 years old, and Atlantic white cedar were removed, mostly to be replaced by red maple, totally changing the ecosystem and greatly decreasing biodiversity. Currently owned by the U.S. government and operated and maintained by the U.S. Army Corps of Engineers, efforts are under way to

*ABOVE RIGHT:* **Black Alder Berries (Ilex verticillata)**

restore the swamp's diversity and bring it closer to its former richness.

The Okefenokee Swamp was also attacked, this time in 1891 by the Suwannee Canal Company in an effort to drain the swamp and access millions of dollars worth of fertile land and timber. Captain Harry Jackson headed this effort, which ended in failure due to financial constraints and an underestimation of the size of the project. This undertaking was thereafter referred to as "Jackson's folly," but the Suwannee Canal Company did manage to extract about 11 million board feet of timber. It further destroyed over another million board feet by girdling the trees but never harvesting them. Fortunately, the Okefenokee survived and is now known as one of the biggest and most primitive swamps in North America. The swamp covers over 600 square miles in southeastern Georgia and northeastern Florida and is a "must visit" for adventurous naturalists.

The pocosins of the southern coastal plains fell under siege as well. Even after the passage of federal wetland protection laws, North Carolina pocosins continued to be destroyed at a rate of more than 43,400 acres a year, most converted to other land uses. Mining these pocosins for peat to produce methanol fuel could result in further losses of these wetlands.

Vast forests of cypress, tupelo, black gum, sweetgum, elm, sycamore, green ash, hickory, oak and other species once covered 24 million acres in the greater Mississippi River Valley. These bottomland forests and alluvial southern swamps were some of the richest forests in North America. The Mississippi River

**Pocosin Wetland, *Alligator River, Tyrrell County, North Carolina***
*Pocosins are considered one of the major regional wetlands of the United States. Although most pocosins are typically composed of evergreen shrubs, some contain a larger percentage of deciduous trees and shrubs.*

and its tributaries deposited nutrient-rich sediments in the floodplain, sometimes from as far away as Canada. This massive ecosystem was bursting with life in its many forms. John J. Audubon wrote in awe about seeing alligators by the hundreds on the shores of the Red River, a tributary of the Mississippi. These forested wetlands were also very valuable in retaining floodwa-

ters. Unfortunately, the forests were cut for timber and the land converted to agricultural use, until today less than 5.2 million acres remain. What is left is fragmented, thus limiting its buffering effects on floodwaters, the effects of which were in stark evidence during the devastating floods of 1993. Furthermore, since we continue to build in the floodways of rivers, we also will

**Pocosins in Spring, *Alligator River National Wildlife Refuge*, North Carolina** *Pocosins provide a crucial habitat for the survival of the region's black bear population. The reintroduction of red wolves to the area in recent years is an attempt to return this predator to its original range.*

continue to pay for the rebuilding of these structures (through the Federal Emergency Management Act), unless we break this cycle of build/rebuild by restoring the floodplains so they can perform their natural flood-storage functions.

Having examined several types of swamps in this chapter, it is easy to see that life in the swamps is prolific: from the smallest of invertebrates feeding on detritus, to a marbled salamander or a hoary bat in an aerial display, to a snapping turtle slowly sinking into the depths, to a dragonfly darting about or a barred owl waiting for night to fall. All these creatures are part and parcel of what makes these wetland systems the givers and keepers of life. In viewing all their intricate interconnections, one message rings loud and clear: it is not possible to change something in my backyard without it affecting yours. The Everglades serve as a striking example of the interconnection of elements in a vast ecosystem of river, lake, marsh, swamp and estuary, of

how the manipulation of water a hundred miles away affects the seemingly distinct and distant estuary ecosystem. For wetlands to survive on this continent, we must awaken to the reality of the interconnectedness of these ecosystems, on the esoteric as well as biological level. With this profound understanding, perhaps then we will insist on comprehensive regulations that acknowledge and protect the web of life.

**Northern Boreal Swamp, Ontario, Canada** *These northern wetlands consist mostly of evergreen trees, including such species as black and white spruce, tamarack, balsam fir and northern white cedar. The canopy in these swamps can be very dense, creating a perfect shady habitat for mosses to proliferate into a mosaic of green across the swamp floor.*

# LAKES

# AND PONDS

*A lake is the landscape's most beautiful feature. It is the earth's eye; looking into which the beholder measures the depth of his own nature.*

- Henry David Thoreau

**T**here are literally hundreds of thousands of lakes and ponds in North America, so that nearly everyone who picks up this book will have visited these kinds of wetlands at some point in their lives. Most likely the visit was a pleasant one, perhaps evoking nostalgic memories of childhood swimming lessons on early summer mornings at the neighborhood pond or of quiet afternoons spent at a secluded lake pensively gazing at gentle waves lapping at the shoreline while pondering the mysteries of life. Whatever personal images are elicited by thoughts of lakes and ponds, most people's direct experience with these water bodies centers around the endless variety of recreational activities they provide. Recreational use may also be the only knowledge people have about these habitats. People tend to use the terms "pond" and "lake" quite loosely, calling a small body of water a pond and a large body of water a lake. In many cases, this description would indeed be quite accurate.

More specifically, a pond is a small, shallow body of water with an even water temperature throughout its depth. A lake, on the other hand, is larger and deeper than a pond, and because of this has different layers of water temperature. In summer, a northern lake's deeper waters may be quite cold while upper layers are warm. This difference in stratified layers of

**Sunrise, *Harvard Pond, Petersham, Massachusetts*** *The fleeting moments of sunrise remind us of how this New England pond changes throughout the seasons: open water greets spring visitors, while floating plants cover much of the surface of the pond in summer. The green colors of summer become the golds and browns of autumn, and winter converts the surface of the pond to a white sheet of ice and snow.*

***OVERLEAF:* Emerald Lake, *Yoho National Park, British Columbia*** *The blue-green color of this alpine lake nestled in the Canadian Rockies is caused by light reflecting off fine rock particles suspended in the water. These particles originate in the surrounding mountain ranges where glaciers grind the underlying rocks into rock "flour" and streams deliver them to the lake.*

water temperatures constitutes the major distinction between lakes and ponds. There are other dissimilarities. Ponds are often shallow enough that emergent plants (whose roots prefer shallow water environments) may grow along the edges or, in some instances, across the entire surface. A pond has little wave action because of the lack of distance across to generate waves. A lake, on the other hand, often has enough waves to inhibit the growth of aquatic plants along some of its shoreline. Dissolved oxygen, the oxygen that has been incorporated into the water and is available to aquatic life, can vary greatly in ponds during a twenty-four hour period. In lakes, this fluctuation in dissolved oxygen levels is more even from day to day. (In different parts of the country, these distinctions between ponds and lakes can become blurred and confused. Many large, so-called lakes, in Florida for instance, follow the patterns of ponds, with daily fluctuating dissolved oxygen levels and with no layered water temperatures.)

Something to keep in mind as we describe pond and lake environments is that they may meld into other types of wetlands, especially freshwater marshes. This means that many of the species of plants and animals discussed in the Inland Marshes chapter are also applicable to ponds and lakes. Red maple, cypress, pocosin, or shrub swamps can gradually blend into ponds and lakes so that it is difficult to determine distinct boundaries. The association of these different types of wetlands with the pond and lake environment provides for a constant exchange of animals, plants, and nutrients, thereby enriching each of the interconnected ecosystems.

Some of our favorite types of wetlands to explore are beaver ponds, in no small part due to that most industrious of engineers, the beaver, maker of wetlands. Modern estimates place the number of beavers in pre-Colonial America at 60 million to 120 million. When explorer David Thompson crossed North America in 1784, he found that the continent "may be said to have been in the possession of two distinct races of beings, man and the beaver," with man occupying the highlands and the beaver in solid possession of the lowlands.

Some Native American legends relate how the beaver was sent from above to create the worlds below, and at least metaphorically that makes sense. Let's examine for a moment how the beaver "creates" a world. Prior to the arrival of the beaver, a stream runs through a forest, flanked by trees and thick undergrowth. The beaver enters the scene and builds a dam across the stream, "chopping" down many of the trees for the dam, for food, and for a lodge. A pond forms behind the dam, flooding more trees, which eventually die, becoming naked snags in the waters of the pond. In a few years' time, the banks are cleared of trees and there is lush, herbaceous growth on the shore and lily pads and cattails in the warm shallow water. Great blue herons, hawks, owls, and other platform-nesting birds build their nests in the dead snags. Wood ducks, flickers, hooded mergansers, and other cavity nesters such as woodpeckers, swallows, wrens, chickadees, and flying squirrels all make their homes here in the dead trees. The waters of the pond become a haven for fish, amphibians, reptiles, otters, muskrats, mollusks, and

**First Light at Beaver Pond, _Fitzwilliam, New Hampshire_** _Early morning sunlight illuminates the tops of these dead snags, while low fog obscures the pond below. Beaver ponds provide excellent opportunities for nesting sites. Great blue herons, for example, construct their nests atop the many tall, dead standing trees surrounded by water, making it difficult for predators to raid eggs or capture young._

_ABOVE LEFT:_ **Northern Pintail (Anas acuta)**

invertebrates. Raccoons search the shallows and banks for food, deer come to eat the young shoots that sprout from the beaver's cuttings as well as other plants invigorated by the new openings in the canopy. The moose arrives to take advantage of new succulent aquatic plants. The mink darts in and out of the water in search of its prey. Coyote, foxes, bobcats, and other predators make their daily visits to the pond looking for potential meals. The marsh hawk and other avian predators circle above. Before long, a whole new world, a whole new ecosystem, has been created by the beaver's activities . A diverse array of life-forms, previously unknown to the area bursts forth from the life of the beaver.

As time passes, the bottom of the pond begins to accumulate sediments, because the water of the original stream slows considerably as it flows into the still waters of the pond. The sediments at the bottom of the pond are enriched and fertilized by the incoming nutrients and become somewhat like a time capsule, waiting to be released by light, air, and oxygen. At some point, perhaps in five or ten years or longer, the beaver's food resources dwindle, requiring the beaver to travel seventy feet or more from the safety of the pond to attain its food. These hardships eventually send the wetland-maker packing. Without the beaver, the pond is doomed. Dramatic change takes place as the beaver dam erodes and the pond slowly drains. The stream appears again as it cuts through the rich sediments. The life inside the time capsule is released and the pond is magically transformed into a beaver meadow, rich with herbaceous (soft-stemmed) plants.

**Beaver Pond, *Southern New Hampshire*** *The bottom of this beaver pond is exposed by lowered water levels. Should the pond remain empty, plants and shrubs will grow in the sediments collected at the bottom, creating a beaver meadow. Other than humans, beavers are the only animals capable of harnessing water for their needs.*

This eventually creates a whole new community for another set of animals, if not reoccupied by beavers. The meadow may later be colonized by shrubs, then trees, back to the forest-type habitat that existed before the arrival of the beaver. The 60 million to 120 million beavers must have wrought a lot of changes in the geography of the world below, diversifying the forest and creating new and different habitats for many different species.

Our model beaver pond may have at first replaced several acres of forest, which contained some fine trees, but what followed was an eruption of life-forms that transformed the forest into an ecosystem with a much higher rate of productivity. It could also be argued that the forest now growing in the alluvial soils is potentially a far more productive forest than the one preceding it. Beaver ponds have other benefits as well. As the water slows down in the pond, the heavier particles drop to the bottom of the pond, so that the water is clearer downstream, and plant communities that eventually grow in the sediment help to stabilize the floodplain.

Another type of pond, far more transitory than beaver ponds, are temporary ponds, also called temporary pools. Often only five to 150 feet across, these wetlands are found almost anywhere in North America, from deserts and sand dunes to woodlands and tundra. Temporary ponds are depressions that are intermittently wet and dry. Some are merely short-lived puddles, solely dependent on rainfall and only lasting a matter of days. Others form in kettle-hole basins left by glaciers,

**Beaver Pond and Marsh, _Birch Hill Wildlife Area, Massachusetts_** _When beavers dam a stream to create a beaver pond in which to build their lodge, eventually the standing trees of the flooded forest die and become snags. These trees provide important nesting cavities for woodpeckers, swallows, flickers, and wood ducks._

retaining water for most of the year, while others are fed by groundwater. Other terms used for these temporary ponds are vernal, autumnal, ephemeral, and astatic ponds or pools.

Although the term "vernal pool" is often loosely used to describe any seasonal pool, strictly speaking it denotes a pool that is filled in the spring and dries in the summer months. ("Vernal" means "relating to spring.") "Autumnal" is a pool that fills in the autumn and usually remains full through the winter. Some pools or ponds fill only for brief periods (one to seven days) during and after rainstorms and may even remain dry for two years or more. These are usually found in deserts and are referred to as "ephemeral" pools or ponds. In

**Sunrise, Harvard Pond, Petersham, Massachusetts** *This pond has diverse flora and fauna. Emergent, floating, and submerged plants all exist here. Fish will often elude their predators by hiding among the abundant aquatic plants.*

the southwestern U.S. they are known as "playa lakes." Communities of crustaceans and aquatic insects with highly developed strategies to overcome long periods of drought have adapted to this type of habitat. Last are the "astatic" ponds or pools, which change dramatically in size and in dissolved oxygen levels, but do not usually go dry. Because of low oxygen levels, temporary and astatic pools cannot support fish, and thus provide a unique habitat for aquatic animals that cannot survive predation by fish.

Temporary pools are a valuable and increasingly threatened wetland ecosystem. Sometimes smaller than the bulldozer that threatens to destroy it, a temporary pool can disappear in the wink of an eye. Disappearing with it is an important resource of food for wildlife in the pool's surrounding area. These pools form important links between the aquatic and terrestrial habitats. When the pool dries, leaves from surrounding trees and shrubs may fall into it or a carpet of lush vegetation might grow there. Bacteria and fungi (decomposers) begin to work on decomposing this material. They and the plant material they break down in turn become food for tiny aquatic insects, mollusks, crustaceans, and worms, which are eaten by salamanders and frogs, all the way up the food chain to reptiles, birds, and mammals. The recycling process here is a continuum whereby the pool recycles terrestrial plants to aquatic plants and animals, back to terrestrial plants and animals.

The survival of many animals is directly dependent on

**Pond and Sagebrush, *Malheur National Wildlife Refuge, Oregon***
*With an average of only nine inches of precipitation annually, water in this high desert basin is a crucial commodity that fluctuates greatly, depending upon snowmelt from the surrounding mountains. The ponds, marshes, and Malheur/Harney Lakes in this wildlife refuge provide a vital migration habitat for birds in the Pacific Flyway.*

temporary ponds. The reason for this in most cases is that these species, or some stage in the development of these species, cannot exist in ponds with predatory fish. Some common inhabitants of temporary pools are wood frogs, spotted salamanders (a type of mole salamander), and fairy shrimp.

Wood frogs can be found throughout most of Canada, Alaska, the Great Lakes region, the northeastern U.S. and in the Appalachian Mountains. This is the only North American frog found north of the Arctic Circle. It is typically some shade of brown with a black mask that ends behind the eardrums, and smooth skin without any markings other than a light line down the middle of the back on some individuals. The lateral ridges down each side of the back are prominent.

We are fortunate to have some temporary ponds near our home, so we have been able to witness these frogs breeding in pools still partially covered with ice. To observe them in their habitat, one must be quiet and patient. They are difficult to see sometimes, but they can be heard from quite a distance. It is a distinctly un-frog-like sound: the vocalizing breeding males sound more like a chorus of quacking ducks.

In early spring, before the leaves begin to appear, if conditions are right, hundreds, even thousands, of wood frogs migrate to their breeding pools, some congregating there within hours of each other, others within a few days. The mating period is brief, with breeding usually completed within two to three weeks. Each female frog is capable of producing 300 to 1,500 eggs, (some estimate up to 2,000), which are usu-

ally deposited in a globular mass attached to submerged branches or twigs. Females return to their woodland habitats immediately after they lay their eggs, followed by the males. In the meantime, the eggs must hatch and the tadpoles develop into frogs before the pool dries up.

The spotted salamander is another species dependent on temporary pools for its existence. They range from south-central Ontario east to Nova Scotia, south to Georgia and west to eastern portions of Texas. The California tiger salamander inhabits vernal pools in that state. Spotted salamanders are stout, six to almost ten inches long, with yellow or orange spots. They vary in color from black or blue-black, to dark brown or gray. These animals also undertake mass migrations to fish-free ponds in early spring. In the North, this occurs from March to April. In the Smoky Mountains, breeding takes place in January and February; while farther south or at warmer and lower elevations, it's from December to February.

In the North, these migrations of spotted salamanders to breeding ponds take place with the first warm spring rains. The female lays 100 to 200 eggs or more in one clear or milky mass two and a half to four inches in diameter. As with the wood frog, these eggs are attached to submerged branches. Within a few weeks, the egg masses may turn greenish from algae. Not all scientists agree, but there is speculation that a symbiotic relationship exists between algae and salamander, whereby the algae supplies oxygen to the developing embryos while the developing salamanders in turn fertilize the algae with their waste products — carbon

*ABOVE LEFT:* **Forget-me-nots (*Myosotis scorpioides*)**

dioxide and nitrogen. Adult spotted salamanders live under the leaf litter in the surrounding forest floor, or underground in small mammal burrows, and are not usually seen. Individuals can live twenty to thirty years. Adults eat earthworms, snails, slugs, spiders, and insects.

Spotted salamanders and wood frogs spend only part of their lives in temporary pools, while others, like some species of fairy shrimp, spend their entire lives in these habitats. The transparent fairy shrimp is one of the more beautiful invertebrates found here. They swim upside down, waving their featherlike appendages. They usually grow no longer than one inch and are very vulnerable to predation by fish, hence they live mostly in temporary ponds. The eggs of these small invertebrates are able to withstand drying, so they can hold over and hatch when the pool floods again in fall or the following spring.

There are many other species found in ponds, from millions of microscopic creatures, including different kinds of protozoa or one-celled animals, rotifers, copepods (tiny crustaceans), and water flies, to all kinds of insects, such as water scorpions, predaceous diving beetles, water boatmen, and the larvae of mayflies, caddisflies, damselflies, dragonflies, and mosquitoes.

Did someone say mosquitoes? Many people donate blood to blood banks, but nobody wants to donate blood to mosquitoes, which, in a way, are the blood bank at the bottom of the food chain. Sometimes we can't help but laugh at the enormous fuss we make over the tiniest contribution that is asked of us. On the other hand, every muscle we move, every gesture we make, every step we take, is not possible without the gift of thousands of organisms donating their lives. In the vast web of life that connects all creatures, a portion of the energy that moves to swat the mosquito was partially donated by preceding generations of mosquitoes.

There are many other types of ponds besides

**Vernal Pool, Jepson Prairie Preserve, Solano County, California** *California contains only 9% of its original wetlands, so the remaining acreage is extremely vital habitat. Seasonal wetlands, including vernal pools, are crucial to migratory waterfowl in the Pacific Flyway. Several rare or endangered plants and animals are associated with these temporary pools, which also function as important flood storage areas.*

the beaver and temporary ponds discussed so far. Some ponds form in potholes left by glaciers, while others may be cutoffs from old river or stream channels. Sometimes a stream will slow and widen into a pond. Here cattails, water lilies, pondweeds, duckweeds, stoneworts, water shield, pickerelweed, and other water-loving plants thrive. Ponds can also be found in the middle of bogs or fens or high in mountains. They may have rocky bottoms, or muddy bottoms where different kinds of sedges grow in the shallows.

Along with ponds, lakes are probably the most familiar of all the wetland types discussed in this book. Natural lakes are created by some of the same forces that shape

**Late Fall, *Sandy Stream Pond, Baxter State Park,* Maine** *This small pond is known by many as a "hot spot" for moose sightings. Emergent, floating and submerged aquatic plants such as sedges, horsetails, waterlilies and pondweeds, provide excellent summer food resources for this large mammal.*

ponds, only on a larger scale. The Great Lakes, Lake Champlain (which forms the boundary between New York, Vermont and Quebec), and thousands of other small and large lakes in boreal regions of North America (including the prairie pothole lakes discussed earlier) were formed in depressions created by the continental ice sheets during the great Ice Age. In the West — most of which was not glaciated by the continental ice sheets — many alpine lakes occupy basins that were either gouged out by the scouring action of glaciers, or created by the damming of streams with debris deposited by melting ice. The Reflection Lakes in Mt. Rainier National Park, Lake Chelan in Washington, and Flathead Lake in Montana are prime examples of lakes formed by these mountain-valley type glaciers. Crater Lake in southwest Oregon, the deepest lake in the U.S., fills a crater nearly 2,000 feet deep and approximately four miles wide and six miles long. It was formed when a volcanic mountain erupted and the cone collapsed into the center. The lake is fed only by rainwater and snowmelt averaging, 66 inches of water a year. Lakes forming in craters normally have rock bottoms and receive a low volume of nutrients, thus they are often crystal clear. Crater Lake is one of the clearest lakes in the world.

Rivers can form lakes, sometimes at their mouths where water builds up behind natural dams and levees. Lakes can also form from receding oceans, or from dissolution. These are sometimes referred to as sinkhole lakes and are most commonly found in Florida and Louisiana. Some lakes are created as a result of the earth's shifting crust, as was Reelfoot Lake in Tennessee after an earthquake in 1811-1812. People have also created lakes for drinking-water supplies, irrigation, hydroelectric power, and recreation. This has often been accomplished, unfortunately, at the expense of existing natural ecosystems.

Aside from these freshwater lakes, there are lakes that are saline in nature, the best example of which is the Great Salt Lake in Utah. It is the second saltiest body of water in the world, after the Dead Sea. Salt levels fluctuate with the level of water, but at the high end of the scale, it has been measured as eight times saltier than seawater. Many of the saline lakes in the U.S. are located in the Great Basin in the West, which includes all of Nevada and parts of Utah, Oregon, California, Idaho, and Wyoming. Others are found in the prairie pothole region of the U.S. and Canada.

Saline lakes are called closed lakes, meaning that water flows in but not out, neither through surface outlets nor through seepage. The only way water leaves is by evaporation. Dissolved minerals are transported by water into the lakes, but since there is no outlet, these minerals cannot disperse and therefore accumulate in the lake. In the case of the Great Salt Lake, it is estimated that as many as 2 million tons of minerals are added to the lake each year. The high mineral content is the reason for the famed buoyancy of the water.

As we mentioned earlier in this chapter, one of the distinguishing factors between lakes and ponds is the difference in temperatures within horizontal layers of

*ABOVE RIGHT:* **Water Arum (Calla palustris)**

water in the lake. Temperature layering occurs in most deepwater lakes in North America. In summer, surface water is warmed by the sun, while lower layers remain cold. Because cold water is denser than warm water, the cold water settles to the bottom and the warmer water floats on top. The waters do not mix and by midsummer, three distinct layers have formed. The upper layer of the lake is most active. Photosynthesis takes place here, and oxygen is produced during the day, causing dissolved oxygen levels to fluctuate, though fluctuations are not as dramatic as they are in a pond.

The middle layer, called the metalimnion, is a transitional zone between the active upper layer and the still bottom layer. Sometimes only a few meters deep, it represents a sudden drop in temperature, which acts as a shield to vertical movements, thus preventing the mixing of top and bottom layers. This contributes to the stagnant nature of the layers in the summer lake.

During fall, as the upper layer cools and the temperatures begin to become more uniform from top to bottom, the layering effect is lessened, allowing for the mixing of the different water layers. This is referred to as the fall overturn. Under these conditions, the activities of aquatic life are more evenly dispersed throughout the lake.

In winter, when ice forms and snow covers the lake, circulation of water layers is again reduced and animal activity is slowed. When ice covers the lake, it prevents the wind from circulating and aerating the

**Whiskeytown Lake, Shasta Trinity National Recreation Area, California** *This lake is one of many in California's Central Valley created by extensive dam projects along the area's rivers and tributaries. These reservoirs provide resources, but have also exacted a heavy toll on the natural wetland ecosystems that were altered or destroyed by their construction.*

water. Snow cover further reduces the availability of light, thus reducing photosynthesis, and in turn, dissolved oxygen. Winterkill, when plants and animals die from lack of oxygen, may occasionally occur.

During spring, as the upper layer begins to warm and the waters of the lake are again exposed to winds, another overturn occurs, allowing the waters and nutrients to circulate. Aquatic life once again begins to disperse throughout the system.

Temperate lakes are more likely to experience these spring and fall overturns, while more southerly lakes will experience an overturn throughout the winter. These changes, caused by differing water temperatures, seasonal winds, and in larger lakes, by the inertia of the earth's rotation, provide for a complex system where dissolved oxygen and nutrients are circulated to a wide spectrum of organisms.

A closer examination of the interplay of elements in the lake environment distinguishes four basic wildlife habitats into which a lake or pond ecosystem is divided: the littoral zone, surface film, open water, and bottom. The littoral zone, or shoreline, extends out from the shore into the lake as far as rooted plants are capable of growing. This is the area where the lake might grade into a marsh, for example, in a protected shallow area such as a cove. The animal and plant life found in the littoral zone are similar to those of the inland marshes described in the first chapter. However, the division of plant communities into zones along the lakeshore may be far more apparent than in an expansive marsh where

**Sunset, Fisher Lake, *Chase Lake National Wildlife Refuge, North Dakota*** *Fisher Lake is a large freshwater prairie pothole lake rimmed with sedges and other plants typical of inland marshes. On the other side of a narrow land bridge lies Chase Lake, a salt lake and major nesting arena for white pelicans that numbered over 19,000 breeding birds in 1995.*

across the whole pond. At the lake shoreline or within the pond, plant zones may grade into each other. Many kinds of protozoans, algae, worms, mollusks, crustaceans, insects, amphibians, reptiles, fish, birds, and mammals find cover, food, and a place to breed in this rich and important habitat.

The second wildlife habitat to consider is the surface film. The unique properties of the molecular structure of water causes it to have a surface tension, creating a film on the water that buoys such insects as water striders, which

there is very little change in water depth. The area or zone closest to shore contains the emergent plants. These plants are rooted to the bottom underwater, with leaves and stems extending above the water. Cattails, rushes, sedges, and grasses are found here. Next is the floating-leaf-plant zone as the water gets deeper. Water lily, watershield, spatterdock, floating pondweed, and other floating plants are common here. Moving further from shore, out into deeper water where light is still strong enough to support plants, we find plants adapted to living under continuously submerged conditions. Some of these include water milfoil, coontail, and elodea. In shallow ponds, the littoral zone may extend

seem to skate on water, zipping here and there in the littoral zone of ponds, lakes, or on the quiet water of streams. This surface film is the edge between two strikingly different worlds, air above and water below. There are plants and animals adapted to living on the surface film or just below it. Whirligig beetles, for example, are often observed in groups, darting about and sometimes bumping off each other, their legs beating 60 times each second. Shiny blue-black or brown-black in color, they are a quarter-inch to half an inch long and have two eyes, which are divided by lateral margins into halves. This split vision allows them to see the world above and below the surface film at the same time.

**Mt. Rainier and Reflection Lakes, Mt. Rainier National Park, Washington** *Mt. Rainier is reflected perfectly in the still waters of one of the aptly named Reflection Lakes. Clumps of red heather (Phyllodoce empetriformis) in full bloom add a splash of color to the lakeshore meadow. These lakes are shallow depressions carved out by glaciers and covered by mudflow materials that avalanched off the mountain between 5800 and 6600 years ago.*

They are able to break through the surface film and dive underwater, bringing an air bubble with them for breathing. These beetles, like the strider, can be found in the littoral zone of ponds and lakes and in slow-moving streams. Other small animals in this unique habitat include water scavenger beetles that come to the surface for air, mosquito larvae that cling to the surface with their breathing tubes, phantom midge larvae, fish spiders, and tiny springtails.

The open water is a third wildlife habitat associated with lakes and ponds. It extends outward from the vegetated littoral zone and downward from the surface to the deeper water where sunlight no longer penetrates. It encompasses free-floating plants and animals, from the microscopic to the fish. Plankton can be found here, stretching across the lake waters and up into the vegetated or littoral zone. Plankton consists of tiny, free-swimming plants and animals. The plants (mostly algae) are called phytoplankton and the animals, zooplankton. Phytoplankton is the indispensable foundation of the food chain and the major photosynthetic producer in the upper layer of the lake. The zooplankton form the first group of consumers as they

**Pine Glades Lake, *Everglades National Park, Florida*** *Located on the westerly edge of Long Pine Key, this small lake is in one of the drier sections of the park. Underlying the park is porous limestone, visible here underwater in the foreground. Limestone is a sedimentary rock made from the shells and skeletons of animals deposited in the seas. It is often very rough, sometimes cavernous, with a pitted surface.*

feed on phytoplankton and detritus and, in some cases, on each other. They in turn become food for progressively larger animals, up the food chain to snakes, turtles, and various species of fish that occupy this open-water habitat.

The amount of algae, and thus the amount of zooplankton, is regulated by the amount of nutrients flowing into the lake. When the right water temperatures combine with an introduction of excess nutrients into a lake, populations of algae can explode, making the waters of a whole lake or pond turbid. These explosions of algae are referred to as algal blooms. In many cases they are caused in part by the dumping or discharging of road runoff, sewage and industrial wastes (all considered to be nonbeneficial nutrients) into the pond or lake, which become food for the algae. Although algae provide oxygen for this water environment, an algal bloom can lead to an oxygen deficit. This occurs when millions of algae die and fall to the bottom, and their decomposition by bacteria, fungi, and other decomposers uses up tremendous amounts of oxygen in the water. As a result, the oxygen-deficient water can cause other organisms, such as fish, to experience sudden die-offs.

Zooplankton are an important food supply for almost all fish of the open waters. A number of fish that feed on zooplankton throughout their lives are sunfish, smelts, shad, herring, and many species of minnows. Other fish found swimming in the open water are lake trout, landlocked salmon, northern pike, lake sturgeon, muskellunge, and many others.

The lake sturgeon (which can grow over six feet long and weigh over 100 pounds) is nearly gone from its original habitat due to dams, overfishing and the pollution of streams it uses for spawning. Lake trout can reach upwards of eighty pounds and may be able to live more than forty years. They were once abundant in the Great Lakes, but when the eel-like sea lamprey found access to the Great Lakes after the building of canals, the impact on the lake trout population was severe. The lamprey attaches itself to its victim and drains its host of its bodily fluids, killing the fish. In the span of about forty years, 90 percent of the lake trout population disappeared. However, this trend is being reversed with the control of sea lampreys.

A more recent disturbance to the ecology of the Great Lakes as well as other eastern lakes, is the advent and spread of the zebra mussel. This exotic (nonnative) mollusk species first made its presence known in 1987 in a small lake between Lake Erie and Lake Ontario. Females are capable of producing up to 40,000 eggs per year, which develop into free-floating larvae. These soon attach themselves to any firm surface, transform into juveniles and remain attached to that site for life. Their rapid proliferation throughout the East has already interfered dramatically with native species by taking over their habitat. Zebra mussels have also caused monumental industrial and economic problems for water-dependent industries by obstructing intake pipes of public water supplies or power-generating plants. One important step in curtailing the spread of the zebra mussel is to educate the public not to

*ABOVE LEFT:* **Common Loon (Gavia immer)**

transport water, plants, or fish from one body of water to another.

At some point, many of the animals and plants occupying the open water die and float to the bottom of the lake, the fourth wildlife habitat under discussion. Here conditions may vary from sand, mud, and rocks, to organic debris, and from shallow waters to deep waters. Many different animals live here, adapting to a multitude of conditions. Trillions of anaerobic bacteria, capable of living in the deeper oxygen-poor lake bottom, work as decomposers. The larvae of phantom midges, gnats, and the true midge are found here as well. The blood worm, the larva of the true midge, is an important food for many fish. Snails, clams, and various kinds of insect larvae make the bottom their home. Bullheads, or catfish, different kinds of suckers, and other bottom-feeding fish search the bottom for algae, mollusks, insect larvae, small crustaceans, and other life-forms. Crayfish, looking like small lobsters, are bottom scavengers. A group of crayfish are

able to devour a whole fish in less than twelve hours.

Ponds and lakes can change over time depending to a great extent on the amount of nutrients being fed into the water body. Ponds or lakes that receive excess loads of nutrients are said to be eutrophic, and are characterized by algal blooms and prolific plant growth. It is common for homeowners who abut eutrophic water bodies to become frustrated with these plants that seem to endlessly interfere with fishing, swimming, and boating. All kinds of methods have been

**Coastal Plain Pond, Nantucket Island, Massachusetts** *The shoreline of this small freshwater pond is colored brick-red by an explosion of microscopic single-celled organisms called euglenas (Euglena spp.) Classified as protists, they have attributes of both plants and animals, and can change from red to green and back very quickly. They usually get their energy from the sun. This particular display was a very ephemeral occurrence: there was not a trace of color 18 hours later.*

employed to eradicate what are called obnoxious weeds. Many of these methods have proved to be toxic and dangerous to wildlife and the environment.

Watuppa Pond in southeastern Massachusetts provides an interesting example of how certain activities impact the eutrophication process. The pond stretches over seven miles from end to end and is about one mile at its widest point. At the turn of the century, the pond was divided in half. The South Watuppa has been developed through the years, with houses lining its shores. Road runoff empties into the pond, and there are industries close by, as well as farms in the nearby watershed. Because of road runoff, failing septic systems, and nitrates from agricultural uses, the South Watuppa is changing far more rapidly than the North Watuppa. It is often choked with vegetation and subject to algal blooms. The North Watuppa, on the other hand, does not have these algal blooms and is not being filled in with vegetation. It is protected by the city of Fall River as a water supply. There are no houses, the city maintains a bordering forest around the pond, diverts road runoff away from it, and does not allow any human recreational access. The two ponds set a striking example of what poorly planned human development can do to accelerate the eutrophication of a pond or lake. It also demonstrates the importance of protective buffer zones around wetlands and, at the same time, makes a powerful statement about the importance of and need for federal wetland protection regulations.

There are countless examples of how necessary and absolutely vital wetlands protection and preservation is for our survival. Not far from our home in central

**Lucky Peak Lake, *Boise, Idaho*** *A dam across the Middle Fork of the Boise River has created this reservoir near the capitol city of Boise. Bordered by rolling hills, the reservoir provides recreational opportunities for swimming, boating, fishing and picnicking.*

Massachusetts lies a beautiful semi-wilderness area called Quabbin Reservoir. This pristine lake is surrounded by miles of buffering forests that help to ensure clean drinking water, plus provide habitats for a wide variety of wildlife species. An aqueduct stretches like an umbilical cord 70 miles to the city of Boston and its suburbs, giving life to the city. Most likely many of the hundreds of thousands of city inhabitants are unaware of their connection and dependence on the natural world. Imagine the shock that would be felt throughout the city and its surrounding area if this umbilical cord were severed. The waters of lakes and ponds nurture not only the human body but the human spirit in myriad ways, and have done so for eons. It seems only fair that we should recognize and accept our responsibility to nurture them in a mutual exchange of life.

**Lake Superior, *Neys Provincial Park, Ontario, Canada*** *In surface area, Lake Superior is the largest body of fresh water in the world at over 31,000 square miles. It is also the deepest of the Great Lakes, measured at 1,302 feet. Industrial, commercial and recreational uses have all shaped the human and ecological history of this vast inland sea.*

*ABOVE RIGHT:* **Pickerelweed (*Pontederia cordata*)**

# RIVERS AND STREAMS

*A man in the woods comes*

*face to face with the creation,*

*of which he must begin*

*to see himself a part.*

- Wendell Berry

The subject of rivers and streams is literally close to home for us. Looking out our east windows, we see a small stream that flows through the forest. Its waters slowly seep through sand and gravel to fill our well. The view to the south is of the Millers River as it winds through north-central Massachusetts on its way to the Connecticut River, ending in Long Island Sound and the Atlantic Ocean. In North America, a river or stream has touched just about everyone's life in some way, directly or indirectly, from a kayaker skillfully maneuvering through roaring rapids to a wastewater treatment plant technician sampling the effluent before it enters the river. Someone operating a computer may be unaware that a dammed river supplies the power to light the screen. Whether we realize it or not, it is likely that somewhere a river runs through our lives.

It is difficult to imagine anything more alluring than a smooth, placid river winding its way into the wilderness, surrounded by the stillness of a deep forest setting. There is a special quality to a canoe gliding slowly and effortlessly through glasslike water. However serene the ambience, not all trips turn out as anticipated, as one of our very memorable journeys can substantiate. Working on a book project on eastern ancient forests, we traveled to the Oswegachie River in the

**Swift River, *New Salem, Massachusetts*** *Streams and rivers serve as important wildlife corridors for aquatic animals such as mink, otter, beaver, and muskrat. The forests and bordering wetlands associated with river and stream banks are an integral part of the wetland ecosystem and provide necessary cover for the movement of many other animals, including foxes, coyotes, bobcat, and bear.*

*OVERLEAF:* **Big Hole River, *near Beaverhead National Forest, Montana*** *This section of slow-moving river meanders along the valley floor in between snowcapped mountain ranges. The slower water allows sediments to drop out and creates a sandier, siltier bottom than in swift-moving mountain streams.*

Adirondacks of New York to explore the Five Ponds Wilderness Area. Also awaiting us was 93-degree heat, 100 percent humidity, a wall of black flies and an upriver paddle. Though we were adequately prepared and accustomed to these situations, a warning seemed to hover in the thick air, "Go back, go home." We ignored these "hints" and, determined, we paddled upriver with steady strokes to our base camp, the black flies taking their toll as droplets of blood appeared on our necks. Despite the annoyances of bugs and heat, we managed to have a good night and spent the following day photographing ancient pines.

On the second night, however, a new challenge arrived at around 11:00 P.M. in the form of a black bear. This in itself wasn't a problem, except that the bear wouldn't leave. Charges at the bear, canoe paddles waving madly in the air, talking to it, yelling, loud noises, a hastily lit, roaring campfire — nothing deterred this animal. Finally, at about 2:00 A.M., we decided that the bear wanted the camp more than we did. We packed up in record time. Exhausted and a bit bewildered, we pushed our canoe into pitch blackness. An overcast sky and heavy fog on the water made our head lanterns useless. We knew two small sets of rapids ahead had to be navigated in the dark. Bone-tired, yet mentally awake, we listened for every riffle, as the sounds of the river came to us like never before. Luckily we held the canoe steady through the fast water and slid through without any major mishaps. The river current eased, and we began to relax a bit as the water resumed its invisible and quiet meandering.

The silence was suddenly interrupted by an animal crashing loudly through the forest directly

▲ **King Brook, *Hawley State Forest*, Massachusetts** *The heavy cover of trees and shrubs provide shade over this stream which helps to keep its waters cool in summer. Cutting this protective vegetation would upset the established balance in the stream ecosystem.*

◄ **Millers River, *Orange*, Massachusetts** *This smooth, quiet section of river provides a suitable habitat to support the growth of these underwater plants: water milfoil (Myriophyllum spp.) and pondweeds (Potamogeton spp.) Water milfoil provides food and shelter for insects that are eaten by fish, while pondweeds are a valuable food for ducks.*

toward us. We heard a huge splash, then silence again. We waited, nerves on edge. Then *Ka-splash!!* The water exploded not more than five feet away. We nearly jumped out of our skins. The "intruder" was a beaver, and thereafter, all the way down the river, beavers kept slapping their tails on the water at our intrusion into their domain. By 3:00 A.M., totally shell-shocked and shattered, we crawled up onto the river bank, crudely set up the tent, and dove into our sleeping bags—to be welcomed and encouraged to sleep by bolts of lightning, rainstorms, thoughts of bear attacks and man-eating beavers. So goes another river journey in the life of nature photographers!

Rivers and streams are defined as bodies of running water. They are most prevalent where rainfall is ample and where evaporation of water from the land is less than the volume of water received through precipitation. Small brooks flow into small rivers, which flow into larger rivers, most of which eventually empty into an ocean, creating a mosaic of waterways throughout the continent. The land area of the United States can be divided into nine major drainage areas or watersheds associated with large rivers. The Mississippi River, the third longest river in the world, has the largest drainage area in the United States (fourth largest in the world), draining approximately 1,250,000 square miles of land, extending from western Pennsylvania to western Montana and from Canada to the Gulf of Mexico. The Mississippi River watershed area is so vast it is often subdivided into smaller units associated with its major

tributaries: the Missouri, Ohio, Tennessee, Arkansas, and Red Rivers. The other major drainages are the St. Lawrence River Basin from the Great Lakes in the United States and Canada to the Atlantic Ocean; the Atlantic and Gulf Coasts from Maine to Florida east of the Appalachian Mountains; the Rio Grande Basin in Texas and Mexico; the Souris River Basin of Saskatchewan, Manitoba, and North Dakota; the Colorado River Basin in Colorado and Arizona; the Great Basin of the arid western states; the Columbia River Basin in the northwest U.S. and British Columbia; and the Pacific Coast Basin along the seaboard from Washington to southern California.

Rivers and streams have some different characteristics that prompt us to divide them into separate categories, but bear in mind that any effort to neatly compartmentalize nature will fail. Many flowing waters retain traits of both rivers and streams and defy our desire to understand them by dividing them. Indeed, to truly understand them is to see their inseparability.

These ecosystems are shaped largely by terrain, velocity of water, levels of dissolved oxygen, nutrient loads, temperature, and type of bottom. Streams crisscross North America from alpine areas to desert and are as different as the terrain through which they flow. A single mountain stream can change radically along its course, cascading down a waterfall, gushing through rapids, collecting at pools—but all variations have fast-moving water. A stream may be called a brook, creek, gill, race, rivulet, runnel, branch, or other names in different locations. If followed to its origin, a stream would

*ABOVE LEFT:* **Wood Turtle (Clemmys insculpta)**

Ephemeral streams may only run during and after heavy rains or snowmelt. A desert arroyo may be a bare trickle most of the year but burst into a torrent during a storm. The nature of a stream can vary widely: one may emanate from a hot spring, another's source may be a glacier.

If a stream originates from an active glacier, the water may be quite turbid from tiny suspended particles of crushed stones and mud known as glacial silt or flour. Many streams, though, have clear water and are fastrunning. Because of the eroding effects of fast-moving water, streams often have rocky bottoms. Fast-flowing waters are saturated with oxygen that is incorporated into the water from the turbulent action of waterfalls, cascades, and rapids. Water temperatures are cool, aided by cold springs, shaded waters, or snowmelt. Cold waters also have the ability to hold more oxygen.

most likely be found to begin at a spring or another source of ground seepage. A spring-fed stream or one that is below the groundwater table is more likely to be perennial in nature, flowing throughout the year.

Let's take a closer look at life in a stream. One

**Kicking Horse River, *Yoho National Park*, *British Columbia*** *The power of moving water is seen here in rocks hewn by the raging currents. It is fed by glacial meltwater streams and small timberline lakes in the Canadian Rockies. The river and its tributaries drain a spectacular landscape that includes mountain peaks, massive icefields, canyons, gorges, cliffs and avalanche slopes.*

meaning they filter their food (tiny algae, animals, and detritus) directly from the currents that drift by. The black fly larvae fits into the food chain as a favored food of trout, which in turn nourishes (among others) people. The larvae pupates underwater inside a seedlike black or brown case, still attached to the rocks. When metamorphosis is completed, the adult floats to the surface in an air bubble and flies away. The biting species of black flies visit many outdoor adventurers, seeking "donations"

of the first discoveries about a stream is that the rocks on which one hops across the stream are extremely slippery. That's because they are often coated with diatoms. Unable to live in the fast current, these single-celled organisms cling to the rocks, making them more slippery than ice. Sometimes one can observe snails grazing on these diatoms. The larvae of the infamous black fly, also called buffalo gnat and turkey gnat, are also found holding on to the rocks. There are 90 species of black flies; luckily for humans, not all bite. At times the larvae are so numerous they form what looks like a black mat on submerged rocks. These larvae are drift feeders,

to the stream's food chain. Nature sometimes has an uncanny recycling system.

Other favorite foods of trout found in stream environments are the stone and mayfly nymphs. Trout eat these insects in both the adult and larval stages. Some types of mayflies have dramatic hatches, taking to the skies in the hundreds of thousands. Roads in some areas can actually become slick and dangerous, totally covered with newly hatched mayflies.

Caddisfly larvae are also a preferred food of trout. There are many species of caddisflies, some whose larvae are found in fast waters and others in slow

**Stickney Brook, *Dummerston, Vermont*** *Snowmelt and rainwater cascade over the rock/gravel bottom of this stream in spring freshet. The forest buffer helps stabilize soils and filter pollutants, while leaves will eventually fall into the stream to be broken down by decomposers. This detritus becomes the bottom of the food chain, supporting life in the stream and the adjoining uplands.*

waters. Some caddisfly larvae are free-swimming and predaceous, but most eat minute particles of plant matter and make portable cases in which to live. Each species constructs a uniquely designed case out of various small objects—pieces of leaves, twigs, grains of sand—which are fastened together with a gluelike substance or silk. The cases vary in shape from tubes to snail-like shells. The net-spinning caddisfly makes a cup-shaped net, which it faces upstream to catch its dinner. The larva hangs out near the net, waiting for its meal to arrive. One is likely to find caddisfly cases in most healthy stream habitats.

Without a doubt, the most fearsome-looking of aquatic insects is the primitive hellgrammite, the dobsonfly larva. The larvae grow to about three inches long and have strong jaws that can inflict a painful bite. An adult male dobsonfly has a wingspan of over five inches. In either growth stage, these insects are easily capable of unnerving people on sight. Hellgrammites can live up to thirty-five months and therefore need permanent streams in which to live. The larvae come out of the water to pupate, crawling sometimes as far as 165 feet upland. Hellgrammites are successful predators and capable of killing small fish and other aquatic animals. They are an important and favorite food of larger fish, and for this reason are prized by fishermen as bait.

When it comes to aquatic life in a fast-moving pristine stream, many people imagine it full of trout. Trout species do well in cool, clean, oxygen-rich waters. Brook trout —"brookies" as some people prefer to call them —

are a sign of clean, healthy, cool waters. They are highly susceptible to industrial, municipal, and agricultural pollution, and because of this, their numbers and available habitats have drastically decreased. Brook trout are native to the northeastern United States and eastern Canada, and were introduced to the West. Other trout species include rainbow, brown, cutthroat, and Apache (or Arizona) trout. Brown trout are nonnative and were introduced from Europe, while rainbows are native to the West and introduced to the east and other suitable habitats. Apache trout is a threatened species found in the higher elevations of mountain streams of the Little Colorado River in Arizona. Other fish found in swift waters include sculpin, blunt-nosed minnow, creek chub, brook stickleback, black-nosed dace, and Johnny darters.

Plants and animals have found clever ways to survive the constant motion of fast-moving waters. Mayfly nymphs and trout have developed streamlined bodies to stay in the current. The water penny has grasping legs and a suction disk that holds it firmly in place on rocks in swift currents. It is so perfectly adapted to fast water that one species is able to survive at the edge of Niagara Falls. Caddisfly larvae of fast waters make heavy casings, and some even attach extra pebbles to each side to weigh them down and stabilize their homes in the current.

Of the bird species that prefer fast-flowing water, the water ouzel or American dipper is the most outstanding in its adaptations to this environment. It is a true songbird, but like no other in North America. Its

*ABOVE RIGHT:* **Marsh Marigolds (Caltha palustris)**

range extends from southern California and New Mexico to Alaska and Alberta. It lives almost exclusively near mountain streams, defying swift currents and frigid water temperatures as it walks (sometimes totally submerged) along the streambed in search of aquatic insects, such as caddisfly larvae and stonefly nymphs. In deeper streams it dives right underwater, foraging for its meals. It may also eat moths, snails, fish eggs, and some small fish. Other birds associated with stream and river environments include the waterthrushes, spotted sandpiper, belted kingfisher, osprey, great blue heron, and many others.

Most mammals associated with a stream environment will also be found using rivers. Various species of shrews, the water vole of the West, star-nosed moles, river otter, mink, raccoon, muskrat, beaver, and mountain beaver are found in these habitats. We discussed the beaver in the preceding chapter. Contrary to its name, the mountain beaver is not a beaver at all; it more closely resembles a large vole and measures nine to eighteen inches long. It often lives along streams. Muskrats prefer marshes but are also found in slow-moving streams and rivers. Mink are very aquatic and use all kinds of water bodies: rivers and streams are no exceptions.

Although all these animals are fascinating in some way, the river otter is definitely the most comical and fun to watch. Given the opportunity to observe them, one would easily be convinced of their fun-loving nature. Aside from their propensity to slide down muddy banks and in the snow, they have been known to

**Rutland Brook, _Petersham, Massachusetts_** _This type of stream provides an excellent habitat for aquatic life adapted to the constant motion of the fast current. Single-celled organisms called diatoms cling to the rocks, creating a slippery surface. Cold, well-oxygenated water is also crucial for the survival of trout and salmon._

_ABOVE LEFT:_ **Narrow-leaved Gentian (_Gentiana linearis_)**

take a pebble, bring it to the surface of the water, drop it, swim under and catch it on their foreheads, then continue to roll in the water, without losing the pebble. They are very capable predators, eating mostly fish if available. Frogs, crayfish, turtles, salamanders, snakes, birds, small mammals, and insects round out the menu. One recent observation surprised us a bit when we noticed an otter with two young on the rocks in the river, upstream from our kitchen window. The movement of the adult dashing onto the rocks then immediately flinging itself back into the water is what initially caught our attention. In the next instant, it was up on the rocks again, this time with what we assumed was a big fish. A bit skeptical that there were any fish that large in the river, we hurried to get binoculars and were surprised to see the adult otter eating a gray squirrel, rear end first (although we did not see what happened to the tail). The young otters tried to get a bite, but the adult was quite possessive with its meal.

When the water in a stream begins to slow down and the stream widens, it begins to take on the characteristics of a river. The water in a river tends to be more exposed to the sun and thus warmer. Fluctuations in water levels in rivers are more moderate, while turbidity and nutrients are usually greater than in streams. Sediments in a slower-moving river will drop to the bottom, resulting in mud, clay, silt, and sand bottoms. These are more common where the river slows at bends, creating sand bars, and at the estuary. If the river picks up speed, a rock bottom is more likely to occur. If it is big enough, and as

**Swift River, *Quabbin Reservation, New Salem, Massachusetts***
*This clear stream flows beneath the beautiful stonework of Keystone Bridge, hand-built in the late 1800's. It is one of the major feeder streams into Quabbin Reservoir, a major public drinking water supply for metropolitan Boston 70 miles away.*

it becomes wider and deeper, a river may be thermally stratified with different temperatures within the horizontal layers of water, similar to what happens in a lake.

Though in places a river may share similar characteristics of ponds and lakes, there are differences distinguishing these ecosystems. The river water is still in motion and has the power to erode its banks. As a river twists and turns, the currents erode the outer banks on the outside of a turn while dropping silt on the inside, slowly changing the river's course. Many tributaries add soils to the river and it may flow dark and muddy. The Missouri River, the largest tributary of the Mississippi River, is a prime example.

Great expanses of river bottom may be covered with silt, sand, and muck, with currents constantly at work shifting the bottom substrates. Few plants and bottom-dwelling animals are found in this endlessly changing world, but where it stabilizes, life immediately takes hold. Freshwater mussels may be found here in abundance. Caddisfly larvae, stonefly, and mayfly nymphs and other insects are also found in this environment, but these species are different than those found in streams. Suction cups, heavy casings, streamlined bodies, and claws are no longer necessary, because most insects in this type of river habitat escape the current by burrowing into the bottom rather than grasping onto rocks. Some, like dragonfly nymphs, may partly bury themselves in the mud, waiting in ambush for unsuspecting prey. Caddisfly larvae living in slower-moving water tend to build lighter cases of small twigs and leaves instead of pebbles used by those in faster

**Missouri River near Ft. Berthold Indian Reservation, North Dakota** *Cattle graze along the shores of the Missouri, the longest tributary of the Mississippi River. From its source in the Rockies, the river flows through the plains to the confluence with the Mississippi at St. Louis. The Missouri is one of the major contributors of silt to the muddy Mississippi.*

*ABOVE RIGHT:* **River Otter (Lutra canadensis)**

waters. Mayfly nymphs have a spadelike snout and pad-dlelike forelimbs for digging into the mud. Those living in the slower-moving water of rivers where oxygen levels are lower, have enlarged gills compared to their relatives in the fast-current streams. The mud puppy, a large salamander and totally aquatic, is a good example of this adaptation. In rivers with low-oxygenated waters, they have long, bushy, well-developed exterior gills, while those in highly oxygenated waters have short gills. Tubiflex worms, relatives of the earthworm, may be very abundant, and leeches, bloodworms, and nematodes also thrive in this environment.

Many rivers and streams once provided sustenance for wildlife and indigenous peoples throughout North America. Unfortunately, like many other wetlands in more recent history, they have been taken for granted and misused as an inexpensive and quick fix to flush our wastes quickly out of sight and out of mind—in some cases with windfall profits that seem to give a sense of prosperity. This prosperity, however, is only a mask hiding our greed. A society that values security only in terms of money earned is shortsighted, bequeathing potential disasters to future generations, for money will not buy prosperity in a land of dead rivers.

With the advent of more clear-sighted approaches, through legislation like the federal Clean Water Act, however, many rivers that once ran different colors for each day of the week now flow clear and clean once again. Federal and state laws exist to protect and

**Salmon River, *Challis National Forest, near Clayton, Idaho***
*Dubbed "the river of no return" by Lewis and Clark, this is the longest free-flowing river in North America. With calm stretches of water as well as churning rapids, it is known for its whitewater trip opportunities and world-class fishing. The fine gravel bottom of the river provides an excellent habitat for the eggs of spawning salmon.*

preserve these waterways to some extent, but these too are subject to changes in political administrations. Industries, municipalities, citizen activists, environmentalists must all work together to restore and improve the conditions of these ribbons of life flowing through our communities. Through rivers we share a common thread: we all live in watersheds, and we all live downstream. Hopefully as we develop a greater sensitivity to the web of life, the trend of abuse will continue to be reversed, and we will learn again to celebrate the gifts rivers and streams provide for all creatures sharing their waters.

If one were to follow a river from source to mouth, it is possible that many of the wetland types we have discussed in this book would be encountered along the way. Generally, slow-moving rivers have coves with adjacent marshes and swamps. In the North, cattails and muskrats may abound there, replaced by cypress trees and alligators in the South. Rivers also flood bottomland (riparian) forests of cottonwood, white ash, sweetgum, overcup oak, and water hickory. The trees provide nutrients to the river, which in turn recycles them back to the land. On its seaward journey, the river eventually begins to feel the effects of tides, and flows through freshwater tidal marshes. Moving farther along its course, fresh water begins to intermix with salt water, entering the estuary, then into the saltwater marshes. The river eventually arrives at its terminus, the ocean.

Water is not static, however, and does not stay in the ocean. It is forever on the move. Every year, the

**Trinity River, _Trinity National Forest, California_** _Aquatic insects have developed adaptations to survive the constant motion of fast-moving water: some have streamlined bodies, others cling to the rocks with suction cups, while some, like caddisfly larvae, build heavy cases to help stabilize themselves in the swift current._

sun's energy lifts approximately 80,000 cubic miles of water from the sea in the form of water vapor. Still more water vapor is given off through evaporation by ponds, lakes, marshes, and through the breath of living beings. All one need do is look to the heavens to see it. A world without clouds would be a world without life. At some point, the water collected in these clouds falls as snow or rain, giving birth to glaciers, marshes, ponds, lakes, rivers, and streams. The water that makes up a large percentage of the human body is the same water that was driven through the tissue of an ancient dinosaur. Which brings us back to the question "Who or what are we?" Rivers and streams, water and light, plants, animals, people — we are all a vast boundless mystery.

**Snowstorm on Tully River, *Royalston, Massachusetts*** *Cold silent waters surrounded by snow-covered banks and trees may convey a sense of emptiness and dormancy, but life continues to thrive: fish and an occasional turtle can be observed swimming; mice or voles scurry beneath the snow. At night, deer and other mammals visit the wetland's edge in search of food.*

In the eloquent words of famed anthropologist and naturalist, Loren Eiseley:

*If there is magic on this planet, it is contained in water...Once in a lifetime, perhaps, one escapes the actual confines of the flesh. Once in a lifetime, if one is lucky, one so merges with sunlight and air and running water that whole eons, the eons that mountains and deserts know, might pass in a single afternoon without discomfort. The mind has sunk away into its beginnings among old roots and the obscure tricklings and movings that stir inanimate things. Liked the charmed fairy circle into which a man once stepped, and upon emergence learned that a whole century had passed in a single night, one can never quite define this secret; but it has something to do, I am sure, with common water. Its substance reaches everywhere; it touches the past and prepares the future; it moves under the poles and wanders thinly in the heights of air. It can assume forms of exquisite perfection in a snowflake, or strip the living to a single shining bone cast up by the sea.*

**Columbia River, *near* Pateros, Washington** *The largest river on the Pacific Coast, the Columbia forms two-thirds of the border between Washington and Oregon. Its source is 1,200 miles upriver in British Columbia. A major waterway for spawning salmon, fish ladders have been constructed to allow the fish to pass the obstructions caused by dams on the river.*

# THE ART

# OF SEEING

## PHOTOGRAPHING
## WETLANDS

*We are as much as we see.*

*Faith is sight and knowledge.*

*The hands only serve the eyes.*

- Henry David Thoreau

By now you realize the tremendous importance of wetlands from the ecological perspective. Wetlands are also productive for the infinite opportunities they provide for the adventurous nature photographer who enjoys the outdoors and is willing to face the elements throughout the year.

Photographing wetlands is bound to include a variety of challenges, from fighting black bear over food in a remote Adirondack wilderness to encounters with swarms of hungry mosquitoes in the steamy Everglades. Whatever the trials may be, the adventure and challenge of photographing in the great outdoors is amply rewarding. The opportunity to spend one's time and to use all one's senses day after day, seeking and waiting for the beauty of nature to reveal itself in all its intricacies, is an unforgettable experience. It's a marriage of the intellect and the senses to be able to recognize that special light, texture, and form, and combine them with the right exposure and composition to capture the subtle beauty of our world. Photographing nature demands that you be visually sensitive, as well as have a mastery of the mechanics of photography.

Even more important is the state of mind that allows you enough physical, mental, and emotional space to be creative. You can go to school and learn how to make a technically perfect photograph. However, this doesn't guarantee that you'll be able to create works of art or to see things in a new and fresh way. I remember showing the image on page 147 to an aspiring photographer. He was excited about the photograph and told me how he wished he could find such a beautiful place, indicating that the only requirement for artistic photography was to be in the right place at the right time. Being in the right place at the right time is important, but even more essential is *knowing* and *recognizing* the "right place" and the "right time."

Nature photography as a form of artistic expression is much more than just recording a scene on film. One of the basic foundations of creative photography is understanding that *what* you see is not separate from *how* you see. "The art of seeing" refers to the quality of attention that you bring to every aspect of your life. It is similar to the attention of a deer in the forest attuned to its surroundings, incredibly present, in the moment. Its nose inspects every waft of air, its ears listen for every sound, capture every vibration, its eyes register every movement. This animal is embracing its surroundings with its whole being. Thus, it is highly sensitive, awake, alive, and present. The deer is fully utilizing its senses. There is little that will escape its notice.

I'm not sure that anyone can actually teach this "art of seeing," however, this is the state of mind of the successful photographer. It is a meditative state of being in which you are fully attentive in each moment. This quality of attention can enable you to see and produce exciting images, while others see nothing worth photographing. Some days I find myself looking for an image that always seems to be just around the corner. I set up the camera, then decide the scene is not worth taking. On occasion, I'll experience a day when I don't take a single photograph. Why didn't I succeed in finding

*OVERLEAF:* **Joe-Pye Weed, Pre-dawn**

interesting images? Was it the light, the wind, the place, or was it me? Maybe I just wasn't *seeing*. It is easy to be distracted by thoughts of the past and future, caught up in an incessant inner dialogue, distracted from the act of being present. Imagine yourself hiking through a tamarack bog where the air is laden with moisture, sweet smells, and the soft sounds of birds filling the air. Moments later, you realize that you are no longer in the bog, but in an upland forest of birch, beech, and maple. You look back down the trail and there is no bog in sight. Your surroundings have changed entirely and you never even noticed! You were caught up in an inner dialogue, but upon reflection, you can't even remember what you were thinking about. You were literally walking in your sleep. It is amazing how we can walk through a forest and not see a single tree, or through the forest of our own minds and not "see" a single thought. How then can we expect to create beautiful photographs?

Nature photography is often described as painting with light. The painter has a palette of many colors and a canvas waiting for the brush stroke of a talented hand. The photographer's palette is nature and light, with camera and film the tools. In order to capture the essence and beauty of nature, there must be an intimacy with it, not as an object, but as a process that is forever changing. The more you learn to see nature, to observe it with that quality of attention that is crucial to "seeing," the more you will be able to combine a creative state of mind with technical know-how to create photographic works of art.

**Joe-Pye Weed, Pre-dawn**

There are many different ways to find interesting scenes to photograph. Sometimes you may encounter scenes that are not very exciting at that moment, but the potential is there. For example, when I first saw the field of Joe-Pye weed it was midday and a bit windy. There was nothing moody or exciting about it. A photographer without the ability to visualize a scene under

**Joe-Pye Weed, Early Morning Light**

differing conditions might not come back, failing to recognize the tremendous possibilities. The more intimate you become with nature, the greater your ability to recognize the potential. The field, about six miles from my house, is a wet meadow, close to a brook, so there is lots of moisture in the area. This meant that early morning cool temperatures could create a ground fog and provide me with the mood I was seeking. A wide-angle

lens would allow me to create the effect of being close to the flowers and, at the same time, give a sense of expansiveness to the entire field. A compass reading confirmed that my view was facing west, indicating I would have a fair chance of getting some color in the sky, which I considered very important for mood. My best hope was to capture a color in the sky that matched the flowers. However, I needed to keep the exposure difference between sky and flowers to where the film would be able to record both. I determined it would be best to take the photo just before sunrise or just after sunset when the contrast in light between earth and sky would be the least. Photographing it in the early morning would mean less wind, but also fewer possibilities for a colorful sky since the view was looking west. I opted to go with the stillness and hope for some color.

I made repeated visits, choosing still, cool mornings for these photography forays. I would get there before sunrise to set up the 4 x 5 field camera. I finally managed to capture the ground fog, creating a moody effect, but it didn't have the color sky I had envisioned. Nonetheless, I was happy with the results (page 147). My shoot wasn't finished, though. I decided to wait a bit longer because I was interested to see how the first rays of early-morning sunlight would transform the scene (above). The two images have a really different feel to them, and although I like both effects, I prefer the pre-dawn photograph. I didn't forget the Joe-Pye-weed field. I returned on several occasions the following year, and one truly magical morning, all the elements fell into place (photo pp. 144-145).

**Birch Hill Wildlife Area, Massachusetts (both)**

It took me a year to realize the potential I saw in that wet meadow. The vision was not possible without understanding the interplay of the natural processes of light, wind, and moisture, as well as the mechanics of composition, depth of field, exposure, and much, much more. It was not just a matter of finding a beautiful place, walking up to it, snapping the shutter, and going home. It was a process of returning again and again—waiting and knowing the right moment—leading up to the final image.

Not all photographs are achieved by this method. I'm more likely to be traveling from place to place looking for a special scene that grabs my attention. This is my favorite mode of photographing:

traveling around the countryside, never knowing where I will find my next image. It might be while hiking along a remote stream, a lonely beach, or a beautiful alpine lake. Whatever the location, the opportunities are endless, especially if you keep yourself open to a wide range of possibilities.

As you develop an attentive and alert eye, you'll also come to realize that a single location can be photographed throughout a lifetime, forever providing fresh and exciting images. The photos above and on page 150 were all taken within a 10-mile radius of my home. The first place is in the Birch Hill Wildlife Area (above), in the towns of Royalston and Winchendon, Massachusetts, and encompasses about an acre or more of a beaver pond, marsh, and old snags (standing dead trees). It can be photographed from three different sides and thus provides various perspectives. The second area I photograph frequently is Lawrence Brook with its adjacent marsh in Royalston, which has one basic

**Lawrence Brook and Marsh, *Royalston, Massachusetts*** *The seasons, weather, and light combine to create radically different images from the same perspective.*

vantage point. The images illustrate how these two locations can provide the opportunity to create strikingly different photographs. As long as I live nearby, I will continue to revisit these habitats. With changing seasons, weather, and light, and aided by a selection of lenses and perspectives, I'm set for years of photographic enjoyment.

Most likely, no matter where you live, there are photographically productive areas not far from home. Whether it's the greenery of a city park or snow-capped mountains, the beauty is there. When picking a spot, there are certain elements that will enhance the opportunities for photography. Water is one major feature to seek out, as it provides countless variations to work with. Smaller bodies of water, as in the Birch Hill Area, are especially important because the water is more likely to be free of wave action, and thus still and reflective. The images you can capture with a mirrorlike body of water are endless. Because of its reflectiveness, the exposure difference between water and sky is also not usually a problem .

Birch Hill has another important element in its favor. The standing dead trees add a very graphic effect to the final image. The trees give a sense of something defined, outlined or delineated. They are dark, clear and powerful—they stimulate the imagination and have the ability to add a mystical or surrealistic quality to the photograph.

When I initially arrive at my chosen location, I look at it from many different perspectives. At first glance, nothing may catch my eye. I wait a bit, giving the images time to appear. I don't want to make the mistake of leaving too quickly. I find that backing away from the scene often helps. I change my focus and look for pictures within the context of the larger scene as well. It's also important not to forget to look down. In some cases, the best photos I've found have been nearly underfoot. Note the image on page 151. The time of day is another important consideration. It's been my experience that the most magical times of day are just before, during, and just after sunrise and sunset. Because the light is low on the horizon, it gives a warmer and more golden tone to the image. The colors are more saturated and vibrant. Midday under a bright sun often washes out the colors, so the images appear drab unless a polarizer is used to liven up the scene.

Once a scene excites me, I have the challenge of translating what I see onto film. I have a vision of what I wish to capture. The beautiful scene and the proper camera equipment are there, but it's my relationship to them as an artist that creates the work of art. I have to determine exactly what it is about the scene that is motivating me. I try to bring all the elements into the picture that move me and discard anything that doesn't. I often accomplish this by changing my position or selecting a different lens. Again, I remind myself not to leave too quickly and not to try too hard. Sometimes it's better not to try at all, but to just sit, enjoy the place, and forget about pictures. When the mind is empty of trying, much more can enter.

I also have to use my technical skills to render the uniqueness of the scene. It's necessary to understand how my equipment works: how the camera and film "see" the scene, how using different lenses and focal lengths alter the image, as well as the effects of different apertures and shutter speeds. I must know how to choose the right exposure, because a difference of one stop (creating a lighter or darker image) can radically change the mood of the photograph. It requires time and practice to become proficient in photographic technique, but learning is part of the fun. You need to take thousands of pictures until, through the process, the camera becomes an extension of yourself. I write down

**Highbush Blueberry Leaves in Frost, *Royalston, Massachusetts***

everything I do: exposure calculation, film, shutter speed, aperture, filters used. When the film arrives from the processors, I check to see what worked and what didn't so I'll know what I did correctly and where I made my mistakes. Eventually, a photographer's eye and the camera's eye share the same vision.

Mastering the challenge of the elements and the technical complexities of photography allows one to concentrate more fully on the task at hand: the thorough enjoyment and experience of the natural world. Simply get out to those wetlands, shoot some film, and enjoy the magnificent outdoors. Become the bobcat stalking the winter marsh, present, alive, and sensitive to its environment. Discard the past and future, empty the mind. When you are in love with the immediate—the flutter of a leaf in the wind, the voice of a yellow-throated sparrow, the thunder of a wave crashing against cliffs at the conjunction of two worlds, a spectacular sunset—when every second is embraced fully, then you are alive, the

*A wide angle lens enhances the perception of depth in this photo of an Atlantic white cedar bog.*

mind is unattached, undistracted, free and receptive —then fresh, new, and exciting images can enter.

In the following pages I offer some technical information on photographing wetlands using specific photographs as illustration. None of the photographs in this book were enhanced, altered or manipulated by computer or color filters. Each of the images was recorded as the film saw it, aided only by the filters that I discuss here.

*Use of a long lens isolates these red maples.*

## CAMERAS

Wetlands offer opportunities from expansive panoramas to macro photography. Ninety-nine percent of the photographs in this book were taken with either a large format Toyo 4 x 5 field camera or a medium-format Pentax 6 x 7 camera. My 35mm equipment consists of an array of Pentax and Canon bodies and lenses, ranging from 20mm to 300mm, but you would be adequately prepared for serious photography with a 28mm, 50mm, 100mm macro lens, and a high-quality 1.4x teleconverter. Two other essential components to your photography outfit are your choice of film and a sturdy tripod. I choose to use the finest-grain film possible (low ISO film). Since I shoot positive film (slides and transparencies) rather than negative film (for color prints), my preference is Fuji Velvia. Using these slow films often requires slow shutter speeds, i.e., long exposures, so a sturdy tripod is a must. I find that many of my photography students are reluctant to deal with the weight and cumbersome nature of a sturdy tripod, but its necessity can't be overemphasized. The use of a good, solid tripod is literally the foundation for technically perfect photographs.

## LENSES

Wide-angle lenses (20mm to 35mm in a 35mm format) are useful in creating looming foregrounds with expansive backdrops. They can be very effective in creating powerful images that pull you into the photograph. The use of a wide-angle lens offers close-up detail contrasted with a broad sense of place created by the expansive background. I used the effect of a wide-angle lens to enhance the lines created by the logs in the photograph on page 152.

Longer lenses, also referred to as telephoto lenses, (80mm and up in a 35mm format), are essential to isolate and/or emphasize certain aspects of a scene. In the larger context of what you see, there are often isolated pockets of details that stimulate the eye. In these instances, I use a long lens to pull images from a distance to the forefront for emphasis. Long lenses are very effective in framing these pictures-within-a-picture, and provide a greater flexibility in creating a variety of photographs from a single location. Proper use of your 100mm macro lens will accomplish this. Putting the 1.4x teleconverter between the 100mm macro and your

*An 81B warming filter was used to keep the snow white and lively in this scene.*

*A polarizer was used to enhance the contrast here between water and vegetation.*

camera body effectively makes it a 140mm lens, adding to its telephoto capability. As a macro lens, it can be used for close-up photography, enabling you to get detailed shots of wetland plants and animals without disturbing potentially jittery and fragile wildlife.

### FILTERS

Although I don't use filters unless I think they will significantly enhance a photograph, there are three types of filters that I find indispensable for certain situations.

I almost always use an 81B warming filter when photographing in shade or on overcast days. These conditions tend to bias the final image toward blue. The 81B is a very light yellow filter, and will disperse the blues and emphasize the warmer yellow tones of the scene. The 81B is especially important in photographing snow. You may have noticed that when snow is

photographed on overcast days or especially in shade on sunny days, it may look blue. Adding an 81B warming filter will keep the snow white.

Polarizing filters are capable of getting rid of glare or haze. They are especially useful in darkening light blue skies and water and in taking the glare off vegetation, resulting in much richer colors. Polarizers work best when you are facing 90 degrees to the sun, otherwise their effect is limited. If you're photographing a marsh and an expansive view that includes a backdrop of mountains that are blurred by haze, try the polarizer. It may cut through at least some of the haze and improve your image. Your polarizer and 81B can be used together to combine the various effects.

Graduated neutral-density filters can be used in an unlimited number of creative ways, as seen in the photos on pages 144, 145, and 147. However, these

*The early morning colors on this beach were captured with the help of a graduated neutral-density filter.*

filters are more complicated to use than the polarizer and 81B and will take some experience to master. A graduated neutral-density filter consists of a square or rectangular piece of glass or resin that is colored a neutral gray at one end. The gray part of the glass is tinted to different densities, stopping one to three times the light going through it. The rest of the glass is left clear, so that light will freely pass through it. Neutral-density filters require a holder in order to attach the filter to the lens. The holder allows you to rotate the filter and move it up and down and to each side.

I used graduated neutral-density filters to produce many of the photographs in this book. These photos would not have succeeded without the use of neutral-density filters. Graduated neutral-density filters are indispensable when you are working with a scene similar to the one shown on the page 156. The sky and ocean are about three to four stops brighter than the coastline. If I exposed the sky and ocean correctly, the rocks and trees would be black. If I exposed the rocks and trees correctly, the sky and ocean would be overexposed. By using the neutral-density filter(s), however, you can have it all

*Dramatic scenes like this one are extremely difficult to photograph without the use of a graduated neutral-density filter. This filter helps balance light and dark areas of the picture so that both retain the details seen by the human eye.*

exposed properly. Basically, you look through the camera with holder and filter attached and pull the gray part of the graduated neutral-density filter over the sky area of the photo, decreasing its brightness. Knowing the right amount of neutral density, just how far to pull it down, and when it will and will not work, takes some practice. Once you have mastered the use of these filters, though, it will increase your options in capturing some technically challenging but spectacular images.